I0797156

Royal Botanic Gardens Kew

# THE BOTANICAL BAR

Published in 2025 by OH
An Imprint of HEADLINE PUBLISHING GROUP LIMITED

1



Cataloguing in Publication Data is available from the British Library

ISBN 9781035422258

Printed and bound in Dubai

HEADLINE PUBLISHING GROUP LIMITED
An Hachette UK Company
Carmelite House
50 Victoria Embankment
London EC4Y 0DZ

The authorized representative in the EEA is Hachette Ireland,
8 Castlecourt Centre, Dublin 15, D15 XTP3, Ireland
(email: info@hbgi.ie)

www.headline.co.uk
www.hachette.co.uk

# THE BOTANICAL BAR

## 50 INTOXICATING INGREDIENTS AND BESPOKE COCKTAILS

ESTHER CLARK &
JENNY LINFORD

## SPRING



## SUMMER

## AUTUMN

## WINTER

# INTRODUCTION

**The next time you sip a glass of wine, enjoy a cup of tea or quaff a cold beer, do pause for a moment to reflect on their botanical origins.**

The starting point for so many of our drinks – both non-alcoholic and alcoholic – is plants. Tea, the second-most consumed beverage after water, is made from the leaves of *Camellia sinensis*. Caffeine-rich coffee – often regarded as an essential morning stimulant – is made from the beans of *Coffea* plants. Fruits – from oranges to mangoes – are used to make juices and cordials, while coconuts provide refreshing coconut water. Alcoholic drinks, similarly, have their roots in plants. As with the food, the history of alcoholic drinks is one of considerable human ingenuity in taking raw ingredients and processing them into desirable, potable forms. While eating is essential to sustain life, alcohol is not. Yet for thousands of years, in societies around the world, humans have valued alcohol and found ways to make it using local ingredients. Alcohol is a mind-altering, intoxicating drug which can lower inhibitions and affect our emotions, creating feelings of happiness and sadness. Historically, because of its capacity to alter consciousness, alcohol has been used in religious rites and for offerings to the gods, known as libations. To this day, special occasions such as weddings, birthdays and anniversaries are marked in many cultures by the drinking of alcohol, the sound of a champagne cork popping from a bottle symbolizing celebration.

Alcohol is created through the process of fermentation, in which microscopic yeasts break down sugars that occur naturally in foods such as fruits, producing both ethanol (alcohol) and carbon dioxide in the process. Wine, made by fermenting grape juice (known as "must"), is a drink with a long history. The earliest evidence we have of winemaking was found in Georgia and dates back around 8,000 years. Over the centuries, many cultures – including the Mesopotamians and the ancient Egyptians, Greeks and Romans – played a role in extending and sharing knowledge of grape-growing and winemaking. Although other fruits throughout history, such as dates and figs, had also been fermented to make alcohol, grapes possessed the right combination of sugars, acids and tannins to create an alcoholic drink that not only tasted good but also kept well when stored correctly. Furthermore, the range of grape varieties, with their differences in colour and flavour, made winemaking interesting and diverse, and grapes became synonymous with wine. The tannic juice of another fruit, the apple, is the starting point for cider. Britain, a nation rich in cider-making history, grows special apple varieties, such as Yarlington Mill, Foxwhelp or Dabinett. These are high in acidity and tannins, and have been cultivated specifically for this purpose.

Beer is another alcoholic beverage that has been made and consumed for thousands of years – and which, in the past, was often regarded as a safer drink than water. The starting point for beer is grain, the starch-filled seeds of cereal plants. Before fermentation

can begin, grain needs to be treated to transform its starch into sugars, which the yeasts can consume. There are a number of ways to do this. In Latin America, for example, a traditional beer called *chicha* is made from maize, a grain that was first cultivated in Mexico. Historically, Inca women chewed the ground corn so that the enzymes in their saliva would break down the starch into sugars and allow fermentation to happen. In China and Japan, rice has long been used to make a family of alcoholic drinks known as "rice wines". In both countries, specially cultivated bacterial moulds are mixed with rice grains so as to trigger fermentation. A third method – one found in Europe – is called malting. This is a process where the grain is first steeped, then germinated and finally, dried or roasted, transforming the grain into malt and creating fermentable sugars. Barley has become the favoured grain for beer-making that uses the malting method because it malts easily and well. In European beer-making, beers were traditionally flavoured with assorted herbs and spices. By the end of the fourteenth century, hops – the flowers of *Humulus lupulus*, the hop plant – had become the favoured option for ales and continue to be used to this day.

Distillation, the process by which spirits are produced, uses evaporation and condensation to separate alcohol from water. To create a spirit, a fermented alcoholic beverage, such as wine or beer, is heated until it vaporizes into steam. Alcohol has a lower boiling point than water, so it creates an alcohol-rich steam. When this hot steam comes into contact with a cool surface, it condenses and reverts into a liquid, containing a high proportion of alcohol. This liquid can, in turn, be distilled, increasing the alcohol levels. Spirits have a far higher alcoholic content than fermented alcoholic drinks. Whisky, for example, is bottled at 40–50 per cent, while wine averages 11.5 per cent. There is a venerable history of distilling among ancient civilizations, including those in China, India and Mesopotamia. The medical school at Salerno in Italy in the eleventh century is credited with playing a key part in the history of European distilling. Historically, distilling took place in a piece of equipment called a pot still, which traces its origins to the alembic used in alchemic experiments.

In addition to the fundamental role of fruits and grains as the starting points for creating alcohol, herbs, spices, fruits and flowers play a vital part in adding aroma and flavour to alcoholic drinks. For example, to make gin, a neutral base spirit is macerated with assorted botanicals, then distilled. While the aromatic juniper berry is the key flavouring for gin, coriander seeds, angelica root and citrus peel are popular additions. However, gin distillers can add many more, drawing on the variety of the plant world for inspiration. Liqueurs are spirits which are often infused with herbs, spices and fruits – think of Chartreuse, Cointreau and Kahlúa, to name but a few. Vermouths are another example where botanicals play a vital role: they are added to fortified wine to aromatize them. Fresh fruits, of course, are an essential ingredient in numerous cocktails, used in a multitude of ways, as in lime juice adding tang to a margarita or strawberries blended to create a delightful daiquiri.

This book celebrates the rich, biodiverse world of plants in drinks. In its pages, you will find the fascinating stories of 50 plant-based ingredients together with 50 enticing recipes for both alcoholic and non-alcoholic beverages made using them. So, let's raise a glass to wonderful botanicals – cheers!

## COCKTAIL SUGAR SYRUP

(Makes approx. 150ml)

300g caster sugar
150ml water

**Use this basic cocktail syrup to sweeten your cocktails and balance out acidic flavours and richer spirits.**

—

Dissolve 300g caster sugar in 150ml water over a low heat. Once dissolved, bring to a boil, then immediately remove from the heat.

Leave to cool and bottle for future use in cocktails. Store in the fridge for up to three months in a sterilized bottle or jar.

# SPRING

b
a

# RICE

***Oryza sativa***

**One of the world's great cereal grains, rice is a staple food for around half the world's human population. Its historic role as an important foodstuff is reflected in the fact that it is a plant rich in legend and folklore. It is likely to have been domesticated in China, where it is such a fundamental food that the phrase "Have you eaten rice yet?" is a greeting.**

There are thousands of rice varieties, though broadly speaking, they fall into two groups: indica (long-grained rice varieties such as basmati) and japonica (stubby, short-grained rice varieties such as Arborio).

In the kitchen, rice is used in many ways: cooked in water until soft and served as a side dish, cooked in stock to make risottos and pilafs, and simmered in milk to make rice pudding. Rice flour, made from ground rice, is used to make noodles, pancakes and an array of baked treats.

Not only is rice eaten as food, but in China it also has a long history of being used to make alcoholic drinks known as rice wines. These are both drunk and used in cooking. In Chinese, a special microbial mixture called *qu* is added to cooked rice to break it down into fermentable sugars. In Japan, sake (Japanese rice wine) is made by fermenting grains of rice which have been polished to remove the bran (the brown outer layer) and inoculated with a special mould culture called *koji*. Sake is regarded as an important and traditional drink in Japan, with a number of ceremonies attached to it. At a Japanese wedding, for example, the newly married couple will share three cups of sake, sipping from each one. At dinner parties, guests solicitously pour sake for each other as an act of courtesy. When it comes to presentation, the drink is served three ways: at room temperature, chilled or warmed. There are also special sake vessels and drinking cups – made from ceramic, wood, glass and lacquerware – in which to serve it, depending on the venue and occasion.

## SAKE AND LYCHEE MARTINI

(Serves 1)

50ml gin
50ml sake
25ml lychee juice
Dash of sugar syrup
Fresh lychee, to serve

This simple, delicate cocktail is a sophisticated way to use sake. The lychee is deliciously floral in flavour, reminiscent of rose and pear. Use a good lychee juice if you can.

—

Stir all the ingredients together, then strain into a chilled martini glass. Garnish with a fresh lychee.

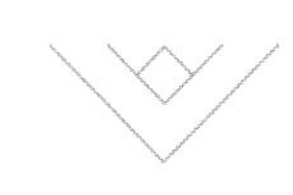

# ANISE

***Pimpinella anisum***

**The herbaceous, white-flowering anise plant is native to the eastern Mediterranean. Prized for its small, fragrant seeds, it has been cultivated for thousands of years. Anethole, the essential oil found in its seeds, gives aniseed its distinctive sweet, liquorice-like fragrance and flavour.**

In herbal medicine, aniseed is prized for its digestive and carminative (anti-flatulent) properties, so is often used in stomach-settling remedies to this day. It has long been appreciated as a breath sweetener. In India, sugar-coated aniseed is served after a meal as a breath freshener. Aniseed is popular in confectionery, as in Britain's aniseed balls or France's *Anis de Flavigny* sweets, and is also used in baking – for example, adding flavour to Germany's *springerle*, those beautifully moulded biscuits which are a traditional Christmas treat, and to richly spiced gingerbread.

Across Europe and the Middle East, a number of anise-flavoured alcoholic drinks are popular, including Greek ouzo or Turkish raki. One striking aspect of this group of drinks is that when diluted with water or ice cubes, they turn cloudy – known as the "ouzo effect". This is due to the presence in the alcoholic drinks of the flavouring trans-anethole oil. Trans-anethole is not soluble in water, so a chemical reaction takes place when water is added to it, and the oil forms tiny droplets in the drink, creating the opaque effect. A shot of chilled ouzo, classically served with ice cubes on the side, is a wonderfully refreshing drink, much enjoyed by holidaymakers as well as locals in Greece.

France produces both pastis and anis, the former flavoured with aniseed or liquorice, the latter with aniseed. To make these, an alcoholic base is infused with aromatics and flavoured with aniseed or liquorice. Among the famous French producers of pastis is Ricard, made according to a secret recipe created by Paul Ricard in 1932. Pastis is enjoyed both in its own right as an aperitif and in cocktails such as a Monkey Gland.

## FRENCH PEARL

(Serves 1)

Small handful of mint leaves
20ml fresh lime juice
15ml simple sugar syrup
50ml gin
10ml pastis
Ice
Mint to garnish

**Refreshing flavours of mint and lime complement the hit of anise you get from the palate-cleansing pastis, which also gives the drink a lovely pearl-like appearance.**

—

Add the mint leaves, lime juice and sugar syrup into a cocktail shaker. Muddle together well. Then add the gin, pastis and ice and shake vigorously. Fine strain into a chilled coupe glass and garnish with a sprig of mint.

# BURDOCK

***Arctium lappa***

**Next time you casually pull apart a piece of Velcro, remember that this useful fastening was inspired by the burdock plant, a member of the Asteraceae family. Burdock seed heads, known as burs, have hooked bristles which grip on to rough surfaces they come in contact with.**

During the 1940s, a Swiss engineer named George de Mestral was inspired to create a fastening for clothing after returning from a walk with his dog's fur covered in burdock burs that stuck tenaciously to the animal. He filed a patent and named it Velcro.

Burdock also has its culinary uses. In Japan, the burdock plant is enjoyed for its edible root, called *gobo* in Japanese, and is eaten as a vegetable. In Britain, young burdock shoots were eaten, with herbalist John Gerard recommending that they be boiled in broth in his 1633 almanac *The Herball*. In British herbal medicine, burdock root, which has a mildly bitter flavour, has long been regarded as a blood purifier and was added to ale as a flavouring before hops (another bitter-tasting plant) were used.

Burdock's best-known use in Britain, however, is in the form of a traditional beverage known as "dandelion and burdock". As its name suggests, this drink combines burdock roots with the roots of the dandelion plant (*Taraxacum* sect. *Taraxacum*), another plant noted for its medicinal properties. The vigorous dandelion plant had a number of culinary uses. Roasted and ground dandelion roots were used to make dandelion coffee, while its leaves were used fresh in salads, cooked as a green vegetable, or infused with hot water to make dandelion tea. Its flowers were used to make dandelion wine, a popular country wine. During the nineteenth century, non-alcoholic herbal drinks, such as root beer, were promoted on health grounds as an alternative to alcoholic ones, such as beer and wine. The temperance movement, which campaigned against the drinking of alcohol because of the social evils associated with it, set up temperance bars, in which non-alcoholic beverages could be enjoyed in a social setting. Among the classic drinks on offer at these establishments was "dandelion and burdock".

## DANDELION AND BURDOCK

**Dandelion and burdock is a favourite of the British Isles. Dark in colour, it has a distinctly herbal flavour with notes of liquorice.**

—

**Non-Alcoholic (Makes 700ml)**

3 tbsp fresh dandelion root
3 tbsp fresh burdock root
1 thumb-size piece of root ginger, peeled and grated
3 star anise
1 litre water
350g dark soft brown sugar

Take a large saucepan. Add the dandelion, burdock root and ginger, as well as the star anise. Fill with the measured water and bring to a simmer. Lightly simmer the mixture for 30 minutes. Turn off the heat and set aside to cool. Leave to infuse for one hour.

Strain the liquid into a clean saucepan through a sieve lined with muslin. Add the sugar and simmer until dissolved. Raise the heat and cook for 5 minutes or until syrupy. Once ready, pour into a sterilized glass bottle or jar. Leave to cool.

Drink the Dandelion and Burdock diluted, as you would a cordial – with still or fizzy water or with a sparkling wine.

# GRAPEFRUIT

***Citrus × aurantium* f. *aurantium***

**The grapefruit is a familiar presence on the breakfast table – served cut in half and sprinkled with sugar in a bowl, or as a glass of grapefruit juice. Yet this large, plump citrus fruit is a comparative newcomer. It is thought to be descended from the pomelo (*Citrus maxima*), the largest of the citrus fruits, and one that is indigenous to Southeast Asia.**

The pomelo is also known as the "shaddock", named after the British sea captain who supposedly introduced the fruit from Southeast Asia to the West Indies. The grapefruit – smaller, thinner-skinned and juicier than the pomelo from which it is descended – was probably created through a process of natural hybridization between the pomelo and the naturally occurring sweet orange of the West Indies. The first potential recorded mention of the grapefruit was in 1750, when Griffith Hughes described a hybrid citrus fruit in his *Natural History of Barbados*, noting it was called the "forbidden fruit" of Barbados.

Nowadays, grapefruits are cultivated in a number of countries around the world, and a substantial amount of the crop is grown to produce juice. Thanks to the presence of citric acid, the fruit has a natural pleasing tartness. However, during the twentieth century, plant breeders in the United States cultivated pink and red grapefruit varieties, which are sweeter and less tangy than white grapefruit, and have distinctive pink-hued juice. It is worth noting that while grapefruit juice is high in vitamin C, it can also interfere with the absorption of certain medicines.

As with other citrus fruits such as oranges and lemons, the grapefruit is prized both for its refreshing flavour and its abundant juice. In the kitchen, grapefruits can often be successfully substituted for lemons or oranges, and are therefore used in baking to create meringue-topped grapefruit tarts, drizzle cakes or cheesecakes. They also work well in fish dishes and salads. In the cocktail world, grapefruit juice is often added to cocktails to provide an agreeable degree of sourness, as in the Paloma and the Sea Breeze.

## GRAPEFRUIT AND BASIL LEAF PALOMA

(Serves 2)

2 tsp runny honey
6 basil leaves, plus extra to serve
Crushed ice
50ml tequila
10ml lime juice
Juice of 1 grapefruit, plus a slice of fruit to serve
Club soda or sparkling water

**The classic Paloma cocktail's hero is bitter grapefruit. This version has added basil for fragrance. Super refreshing and perfect on a spring day, served with lots of ice and club soda.**

—

Trickle the honey into the glass, then add the basil and crushed ice and muddle everything together vigorously with a stirrer.

Add the tequila, lime juice and grapefruit juice, then top up with club soda and garnish with basil and a grapefruit slice.

# COFFEE

**_Coffea_ species**

**Legend has it that coffee was discovered by an Ethiopian goatherd who noticed that when his animals ate the fruit of a certain tree, they became even more lively. That stimulating plant was the coffee tree.**

The practice of roasting and grinding coffee "beans" (the seeds of the plant) and using them to make a drink originates in Yemen during the late 1300s or early 1400s, when it was drunk by members of a religious order to prevent drowsiness.

Coffee seeds are high in caffeine, a psychoactive substance that promotes wakefulness. Today, two coffee varieties – *C. arabica* and *C. canephora*, known as arabica and robusta – are cultivated in tropical parts of the world.

The coffee-drinking habit spread from the Middle East to Europe, where coffee, an exotic, novel, bitter-tasting beverage, was regarded as having medicinal properties. London's first coffeehouse was opened by a man named Pasqua Rosée in St Michael's Alley, Cornhill, London, in 1652. Rosée issued a handbill promoting the "vertue of the coffee drink", in which he describes how it "quickens the spirit", keeps drowsiness at bay and prevents and cures "dropsy, gout and scurvy". During the seventeenth and eighteenth centuries, numerous coffeehouses selling this fashionable drink opened in Britain and they became important meeting places for men to exchange news and information.

The distinctive fragrance we associate with coffee is developed during the roasting process, which creates aroma compounds. From its Yemeni roots, coffee has grown to be drunk around the world. Coffee is enjoyed as a beverage in numerous forms, from the Italian espresso – a small, dark coffee with an intense flavour – to the milkier flat white, cappuccino and latte. Coffee is also a popular flavouring in baking, desserts and confectionery – enjoyed in treats such as coffee walnut cake, eclairs, ice cream and candy sweets. Kahlúa, Mexico's coffee liqueur, is used in cocktails such as White Russians, while an espresso martini combines both coffee liqueur and a shot of espresso, to potent effect.

## COFFEE CALYPSO

**An indulgent coffee-based cocktail made with dark rum and topped with whipped cream. Use a batch of good-quality, freshly brewed coffee.**

—

**(Serves 1)**

**150ml fresh strong coffee**
**Ice**
**25ml dark rum**
**25ml coffee liqueur**
**1 tbsp sugar syrup**
**Lightly whipped cream, to serve (optional)**

Leave your coffee to cool completely. Add a handful of ice to a cocktail shaker, along with the dark rum, coffee liqueur and sugar syrup. Shake well.

Strain into a chilled rocks glass and top with the lightly whipped cream.

# ELDERFLOWER

***Sambucus nigra***

**The appearance of white, lacy heads of elderflower blooms in our hedgerows in late spring is a welcome sight for those who forage for these fragrant blossoms. The flowers of the elder tree have a distinctive, powerful musky scent which lends itself to great and varied use in the kitchen.**

A delightful floral dessert can be made by coating the dainty flowerheads in batter, deep-frying and then serving them sprinkled with a little sugar. Their strength of flavour means that elderflowers are often used as a flavouring rather than a prime ingredient, adding a muscatel note to jams – such as gooseberry, with which they pair very well – jellies, lemon curd, fruit compotes and sorbets and ice creams.

Elderberries – the small, glossy, dark berries of the elder – are also edible, though eaten cooked rather than raw. They mix nicely with apples, adding a hedgerow flavour to crumbles or pies, and can be used to make garnet-coloured elderberry jellies, jams, sorbets and ice creams. They are also used in condiments, including the historic Pontack sauce – said to have been named after a seventeenth-century London tavern called Pontack's Head – a flavourful British ketchup or catsup made by cooking elderberries with vinegar and spices.

Elder trees grow abundantly in Britain and there is a long-standing rural tradition of making drinks both from the blooms and the berries. These include elderflower cordial, a sweet, non-alcoholic drink, which is so popular nowadays that it is commercially produced. Alcoholic "country wines" were also made in farmhouses from elderflowers and elderberries. In Italy, sambuca is distilled from elderberries and flavoured with anise to create a potent liqueur. In the 1970s, there was an eye-catching – and eyebrow-singeing – fashion for serving shot glasses of sambuca, garnished with a coffee bean and set alight! St-Germain, an elderflower liqueur, is a popular cocktail ingredient often mixed with champagne or vodka, both of which showcase the plant's floral notes to brilliant effect.

## ELDERFLOWER GIN TOM COLLINS

Sweet and fragrant, elderflowers are at their best and ready to be plucked from the tree from late May to mid-June. Their heady aroma makes them well equipped for infusing booze. This floral infusion is delicious with lemon juice and topped up with club soda as well as plenty of ice.

—

### FOR THE ELDERFLOWER-INFUSED GIN

10 heads of fresh elderflower
70cl gin
3 large unwaxed lemons, skin pared into strips with a peeler
150g caster sugar

—

### FOR THE COCKTAIL (Serves 1)

25ml elderflower gin, or 25ml ordinary gin plus a 25ml shot of cordial
½ large lemon, juiced
Club soda
Ice
1 lemon, sliced
Twist of lemon

Shake your elderflower over the sink to remove any bugs, then check through the buds for any extra critters and discard any you find. Don't be tempted to wash the elderflower – this removes the pollen, which contains the most flavour. Remove the elderflowers from the stems; this may be time-consuming, but the stems are bitter and will leave you with an unpleasant final taste.

Stuff the elderflower heads into a 1-litre jar. Pour over the gin, then add the pared lemon strips and caster sugar. Make sure the elderflower heads are fully submerged in the gin. Seal and lightly shake, then leave to infuse for one week in a cool, dark place.

After a week, strain your gin through a fine mesh muslin into a sterilized bottle. The gin will now keep for three months in a cool, dark place.

To make the cocktail, measure your gin into a highball glass, top with the lemon juice and stir. Fill the glass two-thirds with ice, then top with club soda. Garnish with a lemon twist and a sprig of fresh elderflower.

# STAR ANISE

***Illicium verum***

**As its name suggests, star anise does indeed resemble a star, with its eight boat-shaped "petals" that each contain a seed. Furthermore, like the spice anise, trans-anethole is its main flavour component.**

Native to North Vietnam and China, star anise consists of the dried fruit of an evergreen tree, which is a member of the magnolia family. The fruits are picked before fully ripe and then are sun-dried, a process which develops the aromatic compounds. In traditional Chinese medicine, it is regarded as soothing to the stomach and good for coughs.

Known as *ba jiao*, which means "eight horns", star anise is central to Chinese cuisine, valued for its warm, sweet, liquorice-like fragrance and flavour. It is one of the fundamentals included in five-spice powder, which is a staple in the Chinese kitchen, though always used judiciously. The fragrant powder is used to create marinades and braising liquid used for proteins like duck and fish. Whole star anise are an important addition to "red-cooked" dishes, in which pork or poultry are slow-braised in a dark aromatic broth. Spicy tea eggs, with their beautiful marbled pattern, are made by simmering hard-boiled eggs in a liquid flavoured with soy sauce, tea leaves and star anise. The famous Vietnamese dish *pho* consists of beef and noodles in a stock cooked with whole star anise. In Western cooking, it is usually used in sweet rather than savoury dishes, offering fragrance to fruit-based desserts such as poached pears or roast pineapple.

In the drinks industry, star anise oil is often used in place of anise in alcoholic drinks such as pastis. The spice's decorative appearance also makes it a popular addition to cocktails, especially those which are served warm, including spiced tipples like mulled wine or cider.

## PINEAPPLE TEPACHE

A pineapple tepache is a low-water, non-alcoholic pineapple drink, in which the otherwise discarded peel of the pineapple is fermented with sugar and aromatics. After sitting for a few days, it will have a slight fizz and a delicious, lightly spiced pineapple flavour.

—

**Non-Alcoholic**
**(Serves 6–8)**

1 large pineapple, washed
2 star anise
1 cinnamon stick
1 thumb of ginger, peeled and sliced
2 limes, juice and zest
150g brown sugar
Lots of ice
Soda water

Thickly slice the rind from the pineapple, then cut the spongy core of the fruit into chunks. Put the pineapple flesh that surrounds the core into a container and store to eat later, and keep the leaves for your garnish.

Take a sterilized 2-litre jar. Stuff in the pineapple rind and core, star anise, cinnamon, ginger, lime and brown sugar. Top up with 1 litre water and seal. Leave to sit at room temperature for five days, opening the lid once every day to release the gas.

Serve with lots of ice, soda water and garnished with pineapple leaves. Store any leftovers in the fridge for a further three days.

# LEMON

***Citrus × limon***

**Bright yellow in colour, the lemon – the fruit of the lemon tree – is a cheerful presence in our kitchen. Where it originates is unknown, but what is certain is that it is cultivated in the warm regions of the world. In Italian villa gardens, there is the decorative sight of lemon trees, in huge terracotta pots, adorning terraces and conservatories.**

Like other members of the citrus family, such as oranges, the lemon is prized for its juice, which tastes sour due to the presence of citric acid and is often used as a souring agent in cooking. Fish and lemon go well together – grilled or fried fish is often accompanied by a slice of lemon to squeeze over it. The Greeks use the acidic properties of lemon juice to create *avgolemono*, a sauce for thickening soups and stews. In Moroccan cuisine, salted lemons are used to add a salty tang to a number of dishes. Lemon juice is often substituted for vinegar in mayonnaise and salad dressings, bringing a brightness to both. The fruit's zest, with its aromatic oil, adds the distinctive flavour of lemons to dishes and is used in recipes from *gremolata*, a zingy Italian condiment, to lemon syllabub. Both the juice and zest are often combined in recipes for sweet treats such as *tarte au citron* (lemon tart), lemon meringue pie or lemon curd.

Lemon juice is the starting point for that simple yet refreshing beverage: homemade lemonade. The fruit also works well in alcoholic drinks. Italy, which is noted for the flavour and quality of its lemons, produces the liqueur limoncello, made by steeping the zest of lemons in spirits. Lemon juice is a key ingredient in a number of classic cocktails such as the White Lady or the Whisky Sour. A lemon twist, freshly cut from a fruit, is a classic garnish for cocktails including the martini, while a G & T is usually served with ice cubes and a slice of lemon or lime.

## LEMON DROP

(Serves 1)

1 unwaxed lemon, finely zested, plus extra for a twist
50ml vodka
25ml triple sec
1 tbsp sugar syrup
25ml fresh lemon juice
Ice

**Lemon is the star of the show here, so use good, unwaxed lemons if you can.**

—

Put the lemon zest, vodka, triple sec, sugar syrup and lemon juice in a cocktail shaker with a handful of ice and shake vigorously.

Strain into a chilled martini glass and finish with a twist of lemon.

# MAKRUT LIME

***Citrus hystrix***

**A member of the large citrus family, the small, thorny makrut lime tree is thought to be indigenous to Southeast Asia. It has been cultivated in this part of the world for so many centuries that its origins as a wild plant are now lost to time.**

The small, rounded green fruits of the tree resemble limes, but have a characteristic knobbly surface. In fact, it is the fragrant, glossy green leaves – which grow in a distinctive pattern of two leaves joined tip to tip on a single stalk and resemble a figure of eight – for which the tree is best known and cultivated.

Makrut lime leaves feature prominently in Southeast Asian cooking, and are sold fresh, frozen and dried, though this last iteration is far less aromatic than the others. Their distinctive aroma and flavour comes from the presence of citronella essential oil and they are used both whole or shredded to add a citrus perfume to dishes. In Thai cuisine, makrut lime leaves are an important herb, deployed in classic dishes such as *tom yam kung* – a piquant prawn soup flavoured with chillies, lemongrass, galangal and whole lime leaves – and finely shredded in tasty fried Thai prawn cakes or as one of the toppings for Thai rice salad. The fruit itself is not very juicy, and the highly acidic juice is used in shampoos rather than in food or drink. However, the use of makrut lime zest is widespread. It is added to curry pastes for Thailand's green curry or jungle curry and in marinades for meat or fish dishes. In the world of cocktails, it is the leaf rather than the fruit which is used. Makrut lime leaf syrups, made by infusing a sugar syrup with the leaves, can be used to create drinks such as refreshing Lime Leaf Mojitos or Gimlets, and the green leaves can also serve as an attractive garnish.

# LIME LEAF AND JASMINE SPRITZ

**(Serves 4)**

2 jasmine tea bags
4 fresh makrut lime leaves, torn
200ml boiling water
5 tbsp soft brown sugar
1 lime, juiced
Sparkling wine

Makrut lime leaves have a distinctly bold and zingy flavour. They work really well in this light and zesty spritz made with jasmine tea. Make sure you get hold of the fresh makrut lime leaves – they have a much more intense flavour than the dried.

—

Put the tea bags into a jug with the lime leaves. Pour over 200ml boiling water. Leave to infuse for 24 hours in the fridge. Once infused, strain into a pan, add the sugar and simmer for 5 minutes to reduce. Remove from the heat and add the lime juice.

Once infused, strain the infusion. Divide the infusion between four flutes and top up with chilled sparkling wine.

# TEA

***Camellia sinensis***

**Tea is one of the world's great non-alcoholic drinks and, after water, is the most widely consumed beverage in the world. It has a long and fascinating history, and has its origins in China. Made by infusing the leaves of the *Camellia sinensis* plant in water, tea has been drunk in China for several centuries.**

Tea contains caffeine and its stimulating effects are an integral part of its appeal; Buddhist monks drank it to help them stay awake as they meditated. It is a drink of huge cultural and economic importance. In Japan, the Japanese tea ceremony dates back to the 1500s, in which the making of matcha (powdered green tea) for a guest is elevated to an art form.

Tea is produced by first withering fresh tea leaves and then oxidizing them; different oxidation levels are the secret to creating distinct types of tea, such as green or black. Other varieties are made by infusing tea with fragrant flowers (as with jasmine tea), with spices (as in India's chai) or by flavouring them with essential oils, as with Earl Grey Tea, which was created during the nineteenth century and is perfumed with oil of bergamot, a citrus fruit.

Tea was once an expensive luxury and, for hundreds of years, China maintained a monopoly on it, deriving considerable revenue from its sale. During the sixteenth century, European countries, notably Britain, began to acquire a taste for tea, and the drink was enjoyed by Europe's upper classes. Great Britain, a colonial power, broke China's monopoly by establishing tea plantations in India, Sri Lanka and Africa. Over time, tea became a more affordable drink. These days, a "cuppa" is regarded as a very British beverage – especially black tea, though it is usually drunk with milk. In China meals are accompanied by small cups of tea, such as jasmine tea, served without milk. Iced tea, often sweetened and flavoured with lemon, is a popular refreshing drink in hot countries. The variety of teas and their range of flavours are a source of inspiration for mixologists.

## BOOZY EARL GREY ICED TEA

(Serves 4)

3 Earl Grey tea bags
400ml boiling water
3–4 tbsp sugar syrup, to taste
130ml lemon juice, plus extra for a slice of fruit to serve
Ice
120ml gin, vodka or brandy

**A good cocktail to pre-mix for a group. Tea will need time to cool down and can be made ahead and chilled. Replace the sugar syrup with elderflower cordial if you have some.**

—

Add the tea bags to 400ml freshly boiled water and leave to steep for one hour. Remove the tea bags and add the sugar syrup and lemon juice. Refrigerate until ready to serve.

When the time comes, fill a jug with ice, add the gin and top up with the ice tea. Garnish with a lemon slice.

# ARTICHOKE

***Cynara cardunculus* subsp. *cardunculus***

**Striking in appearance, the globe artichoke is a tall member of the Asteraceae family (which contains many thistles), a cultivated relation of the wild cardoon. It is not a plant for the faint-hearted or impatient, as eating it requires perseverance! The part of the artichoke that is eaten as a vegetable is its flower head.**

This can be enjoyed in its unopened bud stage, when the bracts (which resemble scales, petals or leaves) are tender. Larger, older artichokes are also edible but require the removal of what is called the "choke", an inedible hairy part within the artichoke. The heart is the most prized part of this challenging vegetable. As the artichoke matures, the bracts toughen, and only their fleshy bases are regarded as edible, so the bracts are pulled off and nibbled accordingly. They have a subtle yet distinctive flavour and were once regarded as having aphrodisiac properties – and prized accordingly. They are many varieties, though the violet artichokes that grow on the island of Sant'Erasmo in the Venetian lagoon are especially highly esteemed and sought after.

Artichokes can be cooked in a variety of ways. In French cuisine, artichoke hearts can be blanched, stuffed, then grilled, baked or cooked in stock and then stuffed. In Italy, the bracts from young artichokes are pulled off one by one, dipped into olive oil and eaten raw. A classic dish from Rome combines new-season baby artichokes and peas, cooked together in stock. Artichokes preserved in oil are a classic antipasti treat, also used in salads and to top pizzas.

Cynar, with a name inspired by the plant's Latin name, is a dark brown Italian bitter made from artichokes. In Venice, Cynar is enjoyed as an aperitif, classically mixed with Prosecco (or white wine) and soda water, and served as a sophisticated spritz.

## ARTICHOKE DIRTY MARTINI

(Serves 1)

1 artichoke in brine
2 green olives in brine
75ml gin
15ml dry vermouth
Ice

Swap out the usual olive brine for rich and salty artichoke in this twist on a classic cocktail-bar favourite.

—

Thread the artichoke and olives on to a cocktail stick. Tip 20ml of artichoke brine into a small jug with the gin, vermouth and ice. Mix together, then strain into a chilled martini glass. Garnish with the artichoke and olives.

# SUMMER

# FIG

***Ficus carica***

**Easily recognizable due to its large, deeply lobed leaves, the fig tree is a common sight in gardens in the Mediterranean region. Originally from West Asia, the fig tree is valued for its plump, bulb-shaped fruit and is now widely cultivated in warm and temperate climates.**

Although we consider figs to be fruit, the fig is not, botanically speaking, a fruit. It consists of a fleshy receptacle called a syconium, which when immature contains hundreds of very small flowers within it. When mature, each of these flowers bears a fruit, so the ripe fig which we eat consists of a syconium containing over a thousand tiny fruit. This intriguing botanical structure gives the fig a particularly soft, luxurious texture which is much appreciated.

Figs have also been valued for their gentle laxative action; syrup of figs is a traditional remedy offered in chemists.

A ripe fig is a joy to eat simply as it is. However, figs also lend themselves to culinary usage. In Italy, sliced ripe figs are classically paired with fine slices of air-cured, salty-sweet Parma ham, a traditional delicacy from the province of Parma, and served as an appetizer. Following the same salty-sweet principle, figs also work well with cheese, either as a pairing or in salads. Fresh figs are a beautiful visual addition to fruit tarts and often called upon to make jams and compotes. The fruit is also enjoyed in its preserved, chewy form. In Britain, dried figs were historically used to make figgy pudding, a hearty steamed pudding made from dried figs, suet and sugar. Nowadays, they are added to granola or gently stewed with spices to make a dried fig compote. Fragrant fig leaves are also used in the kitchen, adding an intriguing note to desserts – like ice cream made from custard infused with fig leaves.

When it comes to cocktails, there are both fig and fig-leaf liqueurs, and fig syrup (not to be confused with syrup of figs!) is a popular addition.

# FIG AND BAY SODA

This drink is best made when the figs are hanging low on the tree – and are therefore ripe and sweet. This homemade soda is utterly delicious thanks to its infusions of vanilla and bay. It can be bottled and stored in the fridge or taken on a picnic.

—

**Non-Alcoholic**

**FOR THE SYRUP**
**(Makes 500ml)**

8 ripe black figs, halved
100g golden caster sugar
300ml water
2 tbsp dark runny honey
2 fresh bay leaves
1 vanilla pod, split lengthways
1 lemon, juiced

**FOR THE COCKTAIL**
**(Serves 1)**

50ml fig syrup
Ice
Club soda or sparkling water

Put the figs into a large saucepan with the sugar, water, honey, bay, vanilla pod and lemon juice. Cover with a large disc of parchment and simmer gently for 25 to 30 minutes. Once the figs have softened, leave everything to cool completely. Once cool, strain the mixture through a sieve. Store the strained liquid in a sterilized glass bottle in the fridge for up to one month.

Put around 50ml of the syrup into a glass, top up with ice, then pour over enough club soda to cover.

# CHERRY

***Prunus cerasus* and *Prunus avium***

**The cherry tree has a special place in our affections, valued for its lovely blossom and beautiful fruit. There are numerous cultivars and, from a culinary perspective, it is worth noting that these include both "sweet cherries" (*Prunus avium*) and "sour cherries" (*Prunus cerasus*). While both types are edible, they are used in different ways.**

For centuries, sweet cherries have been eaten as a table fruit. But sour cherries are prized for the depth of sour-sweet flavour that they bring to dishes. Dark red morello cherries are one of the best-known cultivars of the sour variety, which are used in savoury dishes – such as sauces to accompany game or Persian rice dishes – as well as in desserts, like cherry pie or clafoutis, and in preserves such as cherry jam.

When it comes to the world of alcoholic drinks, it is also the sour cherries, rather than the sweet, that are widely used. One of the most famous is kirsch, a colourless eau de vie distilled from the classic morello cherry. Historically, kirsch was produced in the Alsace and the Franche-Comté regions of France. It is a speciality of Germany's Schwarzwald, the Black Forest region, and used to flavour the region's famous cake – a Black Forest gateau. Maraschino is a historic liqueur, made from a particular sour cherry variety called *marasca* by the Italians. Maraschino cherries – candied marasca cherries soaked in marasca syrup – are regarded as the cocktail cherry. There are a number of cherry liqueurs – made by infusing a brandy base with cherry flavour – often known as cherry brandies, which are a critical ingredient of the Singapore Sling cocktail. In Lisbon, Portugal, specialist bars serve small shots of *ginjinha*, the country's beloved cherry brandy, which is imbued with spices such as cinnamon. Famous producers of cherry brandy include Denmark's Heering, which has produced the liqueur since 1818, and Holland's Bols. As with apricots, the kernels (*noyaux*) of cherries have an almond flavour and these are used to make a liqueur called *crème de noyaux*.

## CHERRY AMARETTO SOUR

Sweet and sour, this cherry amaretto cocktail is rich with sweet cherry, fragrant almond with a sherbet edge from the lemon. Use fresh, pitted cherries if you can; otherwise, frozen work well.

—

### FOR THE CHERRY SYRUP

200g cherries (fresh or frozen), pitted, plus extra to serve
1 vanilla pod, split open
1 unwaxed lemon, juiced
100g soft brown sugar
200ml water

—

### FOR THE COCKTAIL
(Serves 1)

2 tbsp cherry syrup
Ice
50ml lemon juice
25ml bourbon
50ml amaretto
1 medium egg white

Tip the cherries, vanilla pod, lemon juice and brown sugar into a pan with the water. Bring to a simmer, then lower the heat and cook gently for 20–30 minutes, stirring occasionally until broken down. Leave to cool for 30 minutes, then strain the syrup into a sterilized jar, ready to add to cocktails.

Chill a rocks glass in the fridge an hour before serving. Put the cherry syrup into a shaker with ice, lemon juice, bourbon, amaretto and egg white. Shake well until combined, then strain into your chilled, ice-filled glass. Garnish with a fresh cherry or Amarena cherries threaded on to a small skewer.

# STRAWBERRY

***Fragaria* species**

**The tiny, perfumed, scarlet fruit of the wild strawberry have been prized for centuries. This beautiful little fruit features in myths, fairy tales and folklore, often associated with romantic love. In Christianity, the strawberry symbolized purity and virtue.**

Over the years, attempts were made to cultivate the wild strawberry in order to produce larger fruit, but with little success. During the late eighteenth century, it was the hybridization of two strawberries from the Americas – *Fragaria virginiana* and *Fragaria chiloensis* – by French botanist Antoine Nicolas Duchesne that produced *Fragaria* × *ananassa*, the plump, modern strawberry which is widely grown today. Delicate wild strawberries – with their intense, fragrant flavour – are a luxury, sometimes seen in upmarket food shops and on restaurant menus.

With their sweet, soft flesh and pleasing taste, strawberries are often served for dessert simply as they are, perhaps accompanied by a sprinkling of sugar and some cream. Bowls of strawberries and cream have become a signature treat at London's famous Wimbledon tennis tournament. A number of classic strawberry desserts such as Eton Mess (said to have been created at Eton School), strawberry fool and the American treat strawberry shortcake all feature the combination of these bright, juicy fruits with luxurious clouds of soft whipped cream. Strawberry jam is a popular breakfast condiment, enjoyed on toast, waffles and pancakes, and also used in sweet treats such as Victoria sponge cakes and Queen of Puddings.

There is a long tradition of infusing drinks with strawberries. Strawberry wines and liqueurs, flavoured by the fruit, exist in a number of countries. Nowadays, slices of strawberries are often added to sangria, alongside pieces of orange and cucumber. Popular cocktails include the Strawberry Daiquiri and the Strawberry Mojito. It is a fruit associated with the summertime, evoking long sunny days and a sense of leisurely well-being.

# STRAWBERRY AND BALSAMIC MOJITO

(Serves 2)

150g strawberries, hulled
2 tbsp golden caster sugar
½ tbsp balsamic vinegar
100ml white rum
Handful fresh mint, plus extra to serve
Crushed ice
Club soda

**Leaving strawberries to sit in a mix of sugar and balsamic vinegar turns them dark and syrupy. Once blitzed, you've got yourself a delicious puree to add to cocktails.**

—

Roughly chop the strawberries and toss them in a bowl with the sugar and vinegar. Set aside for one hour to macerate. Once macerated, puree in a blender or food processor.

Divide the strawberry puree and rum between two tall glasses. Add the mint and muddle together. Top with crushed ice and club soda, and garnish with mint.

# CORIANDER

***Coriandrum sativum***

**Originally from the eastern Mediterranean and West Asia, the coriander plant is noticeably versatile. Its green leafy stalks form the herb known as fresh coriander or cilantro, while its small, round, dried seeds are the spice called coriander.**

The distinctive, pronounced scent and flavour of fresh coriander is divisive, with some considering it unpleasantly "soapy" and others appreciating its refreshing citrus quality. Fresh coriander is a common culinary herb in many countries. In Thai cuisine, not only the leaves and stems but also the roots are used as key flavouring for curry pastes and marinades. In Mexico and India, fresh coriander is used to make zingy relishes. In the Middle East, one finds *zhoug*, an intensely pungent condiment made from coriander, garlic, spices and fresh chillies.

Coriander seeds have a delicate, floral fragrance with a hint of citrus, making them a popular go-to in the kitchen. They boast a storied history; coriander seeds were found in the tomb of ancient Egyptian boy king Tutankhamen. They are an integral component of Indian cookery, used both whole and ground in dishes and chutneys, as well as in curry powders and spice blends, such as garam masala. In many regions of India, coriander is paired with cumin, and in Gujarat, the two spices can be bought already blended. It is one of the spices showcased in both *bahārāt*, the blend used in the Middle East, and in North Africa's fragrant ras-el-hanout mixture. In Europe, coriander seeds are popular for pickling, while the Germans employ them to season cabbage. In French cooking, the phrase *à la Grecque* ("in the Greek style") is used for vegetables flavoured with whole coriander seeds.

When it comes to alcohol, coriander is a popular botanical flavouring for gins. It is also one of the many herbs and spices used to make the aromatic Basque liqueur Izara, and also features in France's famous Chartreuse.

## CORIANDER SEED AND MINT MOJITO

(Serves 1–2)

1 tsp coriander seeds, lightly toasted in a dry pan
Small handful of mint leaves
2 tsp granulated sugar
10ml lime juice
½ green chilli, sliced (deseeded for less heat)
60ml white rum
Ice
Soda water, to top up

**They may seem like a strange addition to this well-loved cocktail, but coriander seeds are light and sweet in flavour, with notes of citrus. The addition makes for a complex and completely delicious cocktail.**

—

Crush the toasted coriander seeds in a pestle and mortar.

Add the coriander seeds, mint leaves, sugar, lime juice and chilli to a shaker. Muddle together. Add the rum and ice and shake well. Served strained over ice in a tall glass or two smaller glasses, top with soda water and garnish with lots of mint leaves and a few extra coriander seeds.

# PEACH

***Prunus persica***

**The peach originally hails from China, where it is regarded as an auspicious fruit – and one with legends associated with it. In Chinese mythology, the peach symbolizes eternal life. The Jade Emperor, who rules over heaven, feeds the Peaches of Immortality to deities to ensure them eternal life.**

The wood of the peach tree was thought to protect against witchcraft, used to make wands and protective seals. Both peach blossom and the beautiful, plump fruit are much depicted in Chinese art, adorning pictures and ceramics. Peaches can be easily raised from seed; today, the fruit is cultivated in many countries, including France, Iran, Italy and the United States. Alexander the Great is said to have introduced it to Persia, from where it travelled to Europe.

One of the characteristics of peaches is the distinctive fuzzy texture of their skin. Indeed, the Roman poet Virgil wrote of "downy peaches". The flesh within the skin, however, is smooth and yielding, and has a sweet, delicate flavour. Eating a ripe peach, with its juice dripping as you do, is a luscious treat associated with summer, when the fruit is in season.

As well as being enjoyed raw, peaches can also be cooked. One famous dessert featuring the fruit is Peach Melba, created in the late nineteenth century by the famous chef Escoffier to honour the opera singer Dame Nellie Melba. His dish consists of poached peach, vanilla ice cream and a raspberry puree, and has now become a classic. Other sweet treats made from the fruit include jam, conserve and ice cream. In the United States, restaurant menus and family dinners feature peach pie and peach cobbler. Peaches brighten up drinks such as fruit smoothies – paired with bananas and strawberries, among others – and peach iced tea, and are a favourite of mixologists, adding a touch of sweetness to their creations.

## PEACH BELLINI

(Serves 1)

1 large, ripe yellow peach
5ml lemon juice
5ml sugar syrup
Chilled champagne

**Use a good, ripe summer peach here – it will make all the difference. The recipe can be easily doubled or quadrupled if you're expecting company.**

—

Use a small blender to blitz the peach, add the lemon juice and sugar syrup and strain through a fine sieve. Pour into a chilled champagne flute and top up with chilled fizz.

# CUCUMBER

***Cucumis sativus***

**The cucumber plant, which grows as a creeping vine, has long been cultivated for its cylindrical fruit, known as the cucumber. Though *Cucumis sativus* had its beginnings in Asia, it is now grown in large quantities around the world. With their tender skin and crunchy, juicy flesh, cucumbers are usually eaten raw. As they are 95 per cent water, it is not surprising that they have long been valued as a rehydrating snack.**

Cucumber is often served in salads, which, in the British tradition, might see it sliced alongside lettuce leaves, tomatoes and a vinaigrette dressing. Sichuanese smacked cucumber salad is a livelier affair, in which lightly cracked cucumbers are mixed with a tasty soy sauce dressing. In Greece, one classic way of utilizing the fruit is by grating or finely chopping it and mixing it with yoghurt, crushed garlic and fragrant mint to make tzatziki – a mezze dip which is served with pitta bread or fresh crudités. Versions of this delightfully cooling dish are also found in Turkey (*cacık*) and in India, where vegetables, including cucumber, are mixed with yoghurt to make a dish called raita. Because cucumbers are so high in water, recipes often include a stage in which cucumbers are salted, in order to draw out excess moisture before they are used.

In England, finely cut cucumber sandwiches are traditionally a component of an elegant afternoon tea. The fruit's refreshing qualities are reflected in the fact that it is often used in chilled soups. In France, cold cucumber soup is served, while in Spain, gazpacho (made from vegetables including tomatoes and cucumbers) is also served cold, the perfect dish for hot sunny weather. Cucumbers can also be cooked, lending themselves to braising, sautéing or blanching.

In the world of cocktails, cucumbers are appreciated for their cooling quality and delicate yet distinctive flavour – with its slight bitter note – used both fresh and in the form of cucumber syrup.

## CUCUMBER COLLINS

(Serves 1)

¼ cucumber, thinly sliced into rounds, plus extra to serve
¼ tsp peppercorns
50ml dry gin
25ml sugar syrup
25ml lemon juice
Ice
Lemon slices, to serve
Soda water

**Fresh cucumber adds a slightly savoury take on this gin and lemon cocktail. Perfectly refreshing as a summer tipple.**

—

Place half the cucumber and peppercorns into a cocktail shaker and muddle everything together, making sure you're lightly bashing the cucumber. Add the gin, sugar syrup and lemon juice and bash again.

Strain the liquid into a chilled glass, add some ice, lemon slices and extra cucumber and top up with soda water.

# FENNEL

***Foeniculum vulgare***

**Indigenous to the Mediterranean, fennel was known to the ancient Egyptians, Greeks and Romans. In traditional medicine, fennel was valued as a plant that strengthened sight, while in folklore it was regarded as protective against witches. A member of the carrot family, the plant has delicate, feathery leaves and heads of tiny yellow flowers. All parts of the plant are edible and possess an appealing anise-like fragrance and flavour.**

The plant's white, swollen stem base, known as a fennel bulb, is eaten as a vegetable. It has a distinctive, crunchy texture and is often served as crudités, or raw in salads, classically paired with slices of juicy, sweet orange. Fennel bulbs can also be cooked. In French cookery, fennel is frequently used as a bed for baked fish dishes, while Italians serve the simple but delicious dish of baked fennel topped with a savoury crust of grated Parmesan cheese. Fennel flowers and fennel pollen are also used as fragrant garnishes to dishes.

The small seeds of the fennel plant are a popular spice. High in anethole, the same compound found in anise, they are valued for both their digestive qualities and their fragrance. In Bengali cooking, fennel seeds are one of the spices in *panch phoran*, a traditional five-spice mixture, while ground fennel is used in China's five-spice powder, used in pork, chicken and duck dishes. In the Italian kitchen, fennel seeds add their fragrance to baked goods like pastries and biscuits, such as crunchy *tarallini*. Fennel seeds are also used to make *finocchiona*, a classic Italian salami named after the plant (*finocchio*/fennel) that gives this cured meat its characteristic taste.

In both Europe and Asia, fennel tea, made by steeping the leaves or seeds, is a time-honoured aid for breastfeeding mothers. In contrast to its health-giving properties, fennel, along with anise and wormwood, was used in the making of absinthe, an infamous spirit, which was banned in many countries in the twentieth century because of its dangerous effects on the minds and bodies of those who drank it.

## FENNEL SEED AND STRAWBERRY SHRUB

**Non-Alcoholic**
**(Makes 10 servings)**

500g fresh strawberries
500g caster sugar
4 tbsp fennel seeds, crushed
500ml raw cider vinegar
Ice
Sparkling water

**A shrub is a non-alcoholic drinking vinegar infused with fruits. This recipe uses sweet strawberries and aniseed-heavy fennel seeds, which are an ideal match. Shrubs are a great way to use up a glut of fruit from your allotment or a day of berry picking. Swap the strawberries for raspberries or blueberries, if you prefer.**

—

Pick the green tops off the strawberries, then roughly chop the fruit.

Tip the strawberries into a 1-litre sterilized jar and top up with the sugar, fennel seeds and vinegar. Leave the fruit to steep for at least a day or up to one week in the fridge. The longer you leave it, the more developed in flavour it will be.

To enjoy, strain 50ml of the shrub into a glass filled with ice and top with sparkling water.

# ANGELICA

***Angelica archangelica***

**In traditional herbal medicine, this flowering plant has long been highly regarded as a blood purifier and as protective against poison, ague and infectious maladies. Much folklore is attached to angelica – it was thought to fend off evil spirits and witchcraft. As the name suggests, it has angelic associations, and is said to flower on the day of St Michael the Archangel (which in the Catholic calendar is 8 May).**

A member of the Apiaceae family of plants (which was previously called Umbelliferae), angelica is a tall plant, with its flower stalks topped with large umbels of tiny green flowers, reaching up to 2 metres in height. It is found in most temperate regions of the world, hardy enough to grow well as far north as Iceland, and was introduced to France from Scandinavia by the Vikings. The entire plant is aromatic, with a distinctive sweet musky scent.

Glossy green pieces of candied angelica stalk are a traditional decoration for cakes, gingerbread and desserts. The candying of angelica is particularly connected with the town Niort in France, an association dating back to the eighteenth century, when local nuns carried out the time-consuming candying process. Fresh angelica leaves – with their notes of anise and juniper – are eaten as a vegetable in Iceland and used to flavour fresh cheeses, rhubarb, salads, poaching liquids for fish, soups and sauces.

Valued for their health-giving properties and flavour, the plant's root, stalk, leaves and flowers are all used to make herbal tea. The seeds and roots (from which an essential oil is derived) are also used in alcohol drinks: angelica is one of the herbs required for the production of vermouth, and is a major botanical in gin. Famously, it is also one of the components of Chartreuse, the French herbal liqueur made to a secret recipe by Carthusian monks since 1737 and named after their Grande Chartreuse monastery. Originally made for medicinal reasons, the liqueur now has a keen following in the cocktail world.

## ANGELICA ICED TEA

**Non-Alcoholic (Serves 4)**

4 tbsp angelica root tea
600ml boiling water
3 tbsp soft brown sugar
1 large lemon, juiced
Lots of ice
Sliced lemons, to serve

**Angelica has a heady flavour not dissimilar to juniper. It works well, diluted and sweetened, in this refreshing ice tea.**

—

Tip the angelica root tea into a large heatproof jug. Add the boiling water, sugar and lemon juice and stir together. Leave to steep for two hours, then chill in the fridge until cold.

Add lots of ice and some sliced lemon to serve.

# ROSE

***Rosa* species**

**While roses are often thought of as purely ornamental flowers – admired for their beauty and perfume – they are also an important ingredient in the world of food and drink. Among thousands of rose cultivars, the Japanese rose (*Rosa rugosa*) is cultivated for culinary application in China, Japan and Korea, while in the Middle East, the fragrant damask rose (*R.* × *damascena*) is preferred.**

The natural beauty of the flower is reflected in how its petals are used in the kitchen. Fresh rose petals are carefully crystallized or candied and used to decorate cakes and desserts. They flavour fruit-based preserves, such as jellies. In Balkan countries, rose-petal jam is made from damask roses. In India, dried rose petals are used in savoury marinades, while in Iran and Tunisia, ground rosebuds feature in spice blends that find their way into rice dishes, stews, roast meats and meatballs.

Roses are also used to create rose water, widely used as a flavouring. The earliest distillation of rose water has been traced back to Mesopotamia in the third and fourth centuries CE. But it was in ninth-century Persia that rose water began to be distilled on a large scale; the famous physician Avicenna is credited with popularizing its use for food. Rose water adds a subtle perfume to a number of desserts and sweetmeats, among them *loucoum* (Turkish delight), India's *gulab jamun* (sweet syrup-soaked paneer fritters) and *rasgulla* (curd dumplings) and the Middle East's *muhallabia* (a pudding made from using rice flour or cornflour).

Roses are also used in myriad ways to flavour drinks. In the Middle East, rose sherbet, made by steeping rose petals, is a traditional non-alcoholic beverage, served at banquets and regarded as a symbol of hospitality. In Malaysia and Singapore, bright pink rose syrup is mixed with milk or condensed milk to make a refreshing drink called *bandung*. Mixologists use rose petals to infuse syrups or spirits and use these in their cocktail creations.

# RASPBERRY AND ROSE FIZZ

A sophisticated and delicate cocktail, gently infused with rose petals. In flavour, it's reminiscent of Turkish delight – with lots of sharp raspberries.

(Serves 4)

50g sugar
100g water
150g fresh raspberries, plus extra to serve
2 tbsp dried rose petals
Seeds from 1 cardamom pod
1 lemon, pared in strips and then juiced
Chilled sparkling wine or champagne
Sugared rose petals, to serve

Tip the sugar and water into a pan and simmer gently for 5 minutes, swirling the pan to dissolve the sugar. Add the raspberries, rose petals, the black seeds of the cardamom and pared lemon strips. Simmer for a further 5–7 minutes, or until the raspberries have broken down. Leave to cool completely, then remove the lemon.

Once cool, blitz in a high-speed blender until completely smooth, then pass the liquid through a sieve. Add the lemon juice.

Divide between glasses, top up with sparkling wine and garnish with a fresh raspberry and sugared rose petal.

# BASIL

***Ocimum basilicum***

**Though in modern times, it is regarded as a quintessentially Italian herb, basil originates from tropical parts of Asia. It has been cultivated since ancient times in India, arriving later in Europe, and thriving in countries with warm, sunny climates such as Italy.**

In the West, the name "basil" is used for what is also known as Genoese basil or sweet basil. There are numerous basil cultivars, including small-leafed bush basil or Greek basil, Mexico's cinnamon basil, Thai basil and purple basil or opal basil. Basil has a complex, spicy aroma – notes of anise, clove and pepper – with the various varieties ranging in their fragrances, some rich in pepper, mint or camphor. It was regarded as a symbol of love, appearing as such in Giovanni Boccaccio's *Decameron* and, centuries later, in John Keats's poem "Isabella, or the Pot of Basil".

In the kitchen, fresh basil is often paired with tomatoes – used to enliven tomato salads or add fragrance to pasta and pizza sauces. One of its best-known uses in the West is in pesto Genoese, a herb-based sauce from Genoa in Liguria (a region of Italy noted for its basil). Classic pesto Genoese is made from generous amounts of fresh basil, ground pine nuts, grated Parmesan cheese and olive oil. In Liguria, this aromatic herb paste is typically tossed with a pasta shape called *trofie*, slices of boiled potato and boiled green beans. Pesto was traditionally made using a pestle and mortar, but can now be speedily produced in food processors. Commercially produced pesto is now widely sold and consumed.

In both India and Southeast Asia, tiny, soaked basil seeds are used to add texture to drinks and desserts, such as *falooda*, a concoction of milk, rose syrup and ice cream, to which they add a distinctive gelatinous texture. Aromatic basil is also employed by makers of craft gin, while bartenders add muddled basil leaves to their creations.

## BASIL GIN SMASH

**(Serves 1)**

**1 tbsp sugar syrup**
**Large handful basil leaves, with extra to serve**
**2 strips lemon zest**
**1 tbsp lemon juice**
**50ml gin**
**Ice**
**Soda water, to top**

**Fragrant and heady, the Basil Gin Smash is a herbal cocktail that is refreshing in the summer months. You could swap the gin for white rum or vodka if you like.**

—

Put the sugar syrup, basil leaves, pared lemon zest, juice, gin and a big handful of ice cubes in a cocktail shaker and bash with a muddler. Mix in the soda water.

Strain into a chilled tumbler filled with ice and then garnish with a basil leaf.

# SUGAR CANE

***Saccharum officinarum***

**Sweetness is one of the five basic tastes our tongues can detect, and foods that offer sweetness have been prized by humans for millennia. While honey, which is made by bees, was the world's first sweetener, it was supplanted by sugar made from sugar cane.**

A tall grass native to Papua New Guinea, sugar cane is filled with a naturally sweet juice rich in sucrose. Humans began boiling this juice down and turning it into sugar in India over 2,000 years ago. The demand for sugar, which was a luxury for much of its history, propelled cultivation of *S. officinarum* in tropical and subtropical regions, including the Caribbean.

There is a dark side to the story of sugar cane. From the sixteenth century onwards, indentured and slave labour was used in both sugar cane cultivation and sugar production. Millions of Africans were enslaved and forced to work on sugar plantations in the Americas. However, pressure from the abolitionist movement saw European powers gradually outlaw the use of slavery in the colonies. These days, sugar made from both sugar cane and sugar beet is cheap and widely available. Depending on refining methods, there are various forms of sugar, among them granulated, caster and icing. Muscovado is an unrefined sugar which gets its brown colour and strong flavour from the presence of molasses.

Sugar is a staple ingredient in food and drink production and in the home kitchen, widely used in baking, desserts and confectionery. Caramelizing sugar by heating it up until it melts and darkens is a classic sugar-cooking technique that creates the distinctive bitter and toffee notes of caramel. Desserts such as crème brulée and orange caramel feature it, while an eye-catching *croquembouche*, France's pyramid of choux puffs bound together by caramel threads, is a traditional wedding treat.

Sugar is used in both teetotal and alcoholic drinks. Rum, made by fermenting and distilling molasses or sugar cane juice, is regarded as a quintessentially Caribbean spirit. It stars in numerous recipes, from a simple Bacardi and Coke to a Cuba Libre. A simple sugar syrup, made by heating together sugar and water, is a critical building block for many cocktails (see page 11).

## RUM PUNCH

**(Serves 4)**

**2 limes, juiced**
**200ml fresh orange juice**
**150ml pineapple juice**
**1 tbsp sugar syrup (made from raw cane sugar)**
**Dash of grenadine syrup**
**300ml dark spiced rum**
**Lots of ice**
**Maraschino cherries, to serve**

—

In a jug, combine the fruit juices, sugar syrup, grenadine and rum with lots of ice.

Fill four tall glasses with ice and top up with the rum punch. Garnish with a maraschino cherry.

# HIBISCUS

***Hibiscus sabdariffa***

**Also called sorrel (not to be confused with the green herb of the same name) or roselle, the hibiscus flower is indigenous to Africa. During the seventeenth century, it was introduced to Asia and the Americas, and is now grown widely in the warm regions of the world.**

In some regions, its young leaves and shoots are eaten as a vegetable and used as a herb. However, it is more commonly cultivated for its fleshy, bright red sepals (collectively named the calyx), often called hibiscus flowers. These are used fresh and dried to add both colour and flavour to drinks, desserts and preserves. Its taste is similar to cranberries, and features a noticeable sour tang thanks to the presence of organic acids such as hibiscus, citric and ascorbic acids.

When the calyxes are dried, their bright red colour darkens considerably, to a burgundy-brown hue. However, when soaked in a clear liquid, such as water, the flowers tint it a striking scarlet. Its capacity to add colour sees it used in desserts such as jellies, or pears poached in hibiscus syrup. Its natural pectin content means it is used to make preserves, such as jams, chutneys and sauces. However, it is in beverages that hibiscus is most widely used. In the Caribbean, where the plant is called sorrel, the calyxes are used, infused alongside spices such as ginger, cinnamon, star anise, clove and nutmeg to create a fragrant, refreshing drink also known as sorrel. Often, rum is added to create a Sorrel Rum Punch, a popular drink enjoyed at celebrations and special occasions, including Christmas. Dried hibiscus is a popular ingredient in herbal tea mixtures. When it comes to cocktails, hibiscus flowers are appreciated for both their decorative effect and appealing tart flavour, often added to a glass of fizz for a touch of colour or used to make syrups.

# FROZEN HIBISCUS MARGARITA

**The slightly sour yet fruity flower heads of the hibiscus plant are popular for infusing into drinks in Mexico. Here, they have been soaked and are added to a delicious and refreshing frozen margarita.**

—

**(Serves 2)**

150ml water
80g caster sugar
30g dried hibiscus flowers
2 limes, juiced
120ml tequila
2 tbsp agave nectar
Lots of ice
½ tbsp fine sea salt
½ tbsp sugar
1 tsp cinnamon
Edible flowers and an extra lime, to serve

Pour the water and sugar into a saucepan and swirl the pan to dissolve the sugar. Add the hibiscus, bring everything to a simmer, and then leave the syrup to cool.

In a blender, put 60g of that syrup, then add the lime juice, tequila, agave and lots of ice and blitz to a slushy consistency.

Mix the salt, sugar and cinnamon together. Wet the rim of the glass and dip it in the salt mix. Pour in the frozen cocktail, and garnish with lime and edible flowers.

# MANGO

***Mangifera* species**

**One of the best-regarded and popular of tropical fruits, the mango originated in India. It is highly regarded in that country, where it was historically a sign of status and a symbol of wealth, with mango orchards maintained by the social elite.**

Mango cultivation spread from India to Southeast Asia, while the Portuguese are credited with introducing it to Africa in the sixteenth century. Today, it is grown in more than 100 tropical countries, including Brazil, China and Thailand, and led by India, a major grower. There are hundreds of mango varieties, and they vary in size, colour and flavour. Popular mangoes from India and Pakistan include Alphonso, Gir Kesar and Honey, while the Julie is beloved in the Caribbean. Typically, the mango has a large central stone, surrounded by soft, luscious flesh which ranges from yellow to orange. The taste of a mango depends on the variety, but often combines sweetness with notes of pine.

In Thailand, firm-fleshed, unripe green mangoes are grated and tossed with a dressing of chillies and fish sauce to make a tasty green-mango salad. Indian cooks use the fruit to make spicy mango chutney, a popular accompaniment to dishes, often served with popadoms. It's also combined with basmati rice and cashews to make an elegant mango pilaf. However, thanks to their natural sweetness, ripe mangoes are often used to make desserts. Handy tins of its pulp mean that the fruit can be used even when not in season. Mangoes have an affinity with fragrant cardamom and are used in India to make *kulfi*, a rich ice cream with a dense texture. In China, mango pudding, with its soft, blancmange-like texture, is a popular dessert.

Mangoes are not only eaten on their own but also used to make juice, while chunks of the juicy flesh are a popular addition to smoothies. In India, a glass of mango lassi – made from fruit puree mixed with yoghurt or buttermilk – is a quintessential beverage. In the world of cocktails, hit mango creations include Mango Daiquiris, Margaritas and Mojitos.

# MANGO MARGARITA

(Serves 2)

1 small, ripe mango
60ml tequila
30ml Cointreau
30ml lime juice
½ tsp agave
Ice
Tajin, for rim of the glass, or make your own mix (below)

—

### SALTY-SPICY MIX FOR THE RIM

1 tsp flaky sea salt
½ tsp chilli flakes or powder
½ lime, zest only

½ lime, cut into wedges, to serve
Chilli slice, to serve

**The quality of your mango will make a world of difference here. A good, ripe Alphonso mango is perfect for this. The flesh should be bright and taste sweet.**

—

Blitz the mango flesh in a blender until smooth and add to a cocktail shaker. Add the tequila, Cointreau, lime juice and agave. Top with ice and shake well.

Rub the rim of two chilled short glasses with a lime wedge before dipping in the Tajin or your own salty-spicy mix. Fill the glasses with ice two-thirds of the way. Pour the strained cocktail into them and garnish with lime and a chilli slice.

# TOMATO

***Solanum lycopersicum***

**The juicy, rounded, edible fruits of the tomato plant are a familiar sight in kitchens throughout the world. Native to Peru, the tomato quickly spread to much of South and Central America, and has since travelled worldwide, becoming a widely cultivated and consumed fruit.**

Following their conquest of Central America, the Spanish introduced the tomato to Europe in the sixteenth century. Its resemblance to deadly nightshade (both plants are members of the same botanical family, Solanaceae) meant that the exotic new arrival was at first regarded with wariness and initially grown as an ornamental plant rather than a culinary one. Among the folklore attached to it was the idea that it possessed aphrodisiac qualities, hence its French name *pomme d'amour*, meaning "love apple", a name by which it was known in Britain. It was also linked to the mythological Garden of Hesperides, with the Italians calling it *pomodoro* ("golden apple").

Over time, the tomato started to be used in the kitchen, but its acceptance was a gradual process. One notable champion of the tomato as an ingredient was the American President Thomas Jefferson. One popular story is that Jefferson consumed a tomato in public in Lynchburg, Virginia, to demonstrate that it was safe to eat. Today, of course, the tomato, with its intriguing combination of sweetness and acidity, is eaten in numerous forms – among them is the popular condiment ketchup. The fruit is often thought of as a quintessentially Mediterranean ingredient; it features in classic Italian dishes, from pasta sauces to pizza. Botanically speaking, the tomato is a berry, but from a culinary perspective, it is viewed as a vegetable. In the United States, a 1893 Supreme Court ruling on the *Nix v. Hedden* case ruled that the tomato was to be legally considered a vegetable.

Consisting of around 95 per cent water, tomatoes are not just eaten in their solid form. They are processed and converted into a drink: red, velvety tomato juice. During the 1920s or 1930s, a new cocktail made using tomato juice and vodka was created, although who first came up with it and where is disputed. To this day, the Bloody Mary remains a wildly popular tipple.

## BLOODY MARY

**Use a glut of fresh tomatoes in this recipe for the ultimate Bloody Mary. Pass the tomatoes through a juicer and strain well before using.**

—

**(Serves 1)**

**Ice**
**50ml vodka**
**200ml fresh tomato juice**
**¼ tsp celery salt**
**¼ tsp brown sugar**
**Pinch black pepper**
**Few shakes Worcestershire sauce**
**Few shakes Tabasco**
**Queen (or Gordal) green olives, lemon wedges, leafy celery sticks and Aleppo pepper, to serve**

Fill your glass with ice cubes. Add the vodka and tomato juice. Stir in the celery salt, brown sugar, black pepper, Worcestershire sauce and Tabasco.

Thread olives on to a cocktail stick and use to garnish the Bloody Mary along with lemon wedges, celery and a pinch of Aleppo chilli pepper flakes.

# MINT

***Mentha*** **species**

**Toothpaste, chewing gum, sweets, cough medicine, air freshener – all of these feature mint. It is a remarkably versatile herb, widely cultivated and valued for both its pronounced, clean, refreshing aroma and its flavour. The genus *Mentha* contains a number of species.**

Among the best known of these are spearmint (*M. spicata*) and peppermint (*M.* × *piperita*), but there are many others, including Moroccan mint (*M. spicata* var. *crispa* "Moroccan") and basil mint (*M.* × *piperita* f. *citrata* "Basil"). Peppermint is high in menthol, which creates a cooling sensation in the mouth.

Spearmint, also known as garden mint, is used as a culinary herb in a number of ways. In British cuisine, mint sauce – made from mixing the fresh herb with vinegar and sugar – and mint jelly are both classic accompaniments for roast lamb, the fragrant herb slicing through the richness of the meat. Sprigs of mint added to new potatoes or garden peas as they boil are another traditional use. In the Middle East, chopped fresh mint leaves enliven tabbouleh (parsley and bulgur wheat salad), while dried mint is a popular flavouring in Greek cuisine, used in dishes such as tzatziki, a cucumber and yoghurt dip. Peppermint oil is widely used in confectionery, adding its aroma to chocolate, fondant filling, sweets and cookies.

Mint teas, made with either fresh or dried leaves, have been touted for their digestive properties and are often enjoyed after a meal for that reason. In Morocco, mint tea is made with abundant quantities of the fresh herb, sweetened with sugar and served in dainty glasses. If you seek something stronger, crème de menthe, a sweet green liqueur, is employed to make a cocktail called a Grasshopper. But the most famous mint drink with alcohol is the Mint Julep. Made from fresh mint, bourbon, sugar syrup and crushed ice, this creation originated in the southern states of the US and is particularly associated with the famous Kentucky Derby horse race, where several thousand Mint Juleps are served each year.

## MINT JULEP

**(Serves 1)**

**Big handful fresh mint (around 12 large mint leaves), plus extra to serve**

**60ml bourbon**

**30ml sugar syrup**

**2–3 dashes angostura bitters**

**Ice**

**This classic mint cocktail is super refreshing. It's famed for its cool, crisp taste, with the mint complementing the rich bourbon.**

—

Roughly chop the mint leaves and muddle vigorously in a cocktail shaker. Add the bourbon, sugar syrup and bitters and fill with ice. Shake well.

Fill a cold highball with crushed ice and a big sprig of mint. Strain the cocktail into the glass over the ice.

# WATERMELON

***Citrullus lanatus***

**A member of the gourd family, the splendid, large, rounded watermelon – with its eye-catching pink flesh – is striking. As its name suggests, the fruit consists of 92 per cent water and it is known for its thirst-quenching properties.**

The fact that it could be transported and stored made it a useful and portable source of liquid. Watermelons probably originated in Africa; they grow well in both tropical and temperate climates. Human beings are long-standing fans: we cultivated the fruit in Egypt over 4,000 years ago. Over time, hundreds of watermelon cultivars have been developed.

On a hot summer's day, a juicy slice of chilled watermelon is a simple and refreshing treat, an easy but delicious way to round off a meal. Seeing how far one can spit the glossy black pips is a game which has amused generations of children (and adults). Nowadays, though, seedless watermelons are increasingly available. Their seeds are, in fact, edible, and roasted, are a popular snack. Pieces of watermelon mixed with chunks of salty feta cheese is a delicious, no-frills salad. The rind of the fruit can also be eaten – watermelon rind pickle is a recipe with its roots in the American South. In Sicily, a traditional pudding called *gelo di melone* is made from watermelon juice, thickened with cornstarch and flavoured with cinnamon and jasmine flowers. Icy watermelon granita is another classic Sicilian treat made using the fruit.

With its pretty pink colour and high water content, the watermelon lends itself to use in refreshments. One such appealing summery cocktail is the Watermelon Daiquiri, made from rum, watermelon flesh and watermelon liqueur. An eye-catching party piece can be made by piercing a whole watermelon, pouring vodka into the fruit and serving slices of the alcohol-infused fruit to guests.

## WATERMELON AND POMEGRANATE PUNCH

**(Serves 8)**

**1 medium watermelon, cut into chunks**

**2 pomegranates, cut into quarters and skin removed**

**6 limes, juiced, plus extra for lime wedges to serve**

**1 small bunch mint, plus extra to serve**

**200ml gin**

**50ml sugar syrup**

**4 dashes angostura bitters**

**Lots of ice**

**This cocktail is great for a crowd. Make a batch and serve at the table with a tower of glasses and plenty of ice.**

—

Cut the watermelon and remove rind. Separate the pomegranate seeds away from the fruit's thick skin. Put the watermelon chunks and pomegranate seeds into a juicer, then add the lime juice and mint leaves.

Chill the juice in a large jug. Once cold, mix with the gin and sugar syrup as well as the bitters. Pour into a punch bowl and serve with lots of ice, lime wedges, pomegranate and mint.

# AUTUMN

# GRAPE

***Vitis vinifera***

**For millennia, humans have cultivated grapevines, growing them in vineyards and harvesting their bunches of juicy fruit. Grapes have been and remain an important crop, valued not just for eating but also because wine can be made from their juice.**

Native to the Mediterranean region, the grape is rich in religious and cultural significance. Vines, grapes and winemaking were depicted on tomb walls in ancient Egypt. In Greek mythology, Dionysus, the god of fertility, is said to have taught winemaking to humanity, and in later traditions was also the god of wine and pleasure. Wine, with its capacity to alter consciousness, has long been used in religious ceremonies and is central to both Judaism and Christianity.

*Vitis vinifera* is a versatile plant with many uses in the kitchen. Its large leaves, fresh or in brine, are used as an edible wrapper for fillings of rice and meat in dishes such as Greek *dolmades*. There are numerous varieties of the fruit, grown both as table grapes and for winemaking. The muscat grape, valued for its perfume, is both eaten and used to make wines such as Italy's Moscato d'Asti. Fresh grapes are used in cooking in both savoury and sweet dishes. They are also widely eaten in their dried form: raisins, sultanas (made from sultana grapes) and currants (the name for dried Corinth grapes). These preserved fruits play a special part in baking, and contribute to traditional delicacies such as mince pies, Christmas cake and currant buns.

The history of winemaking is ancient and fascinating. Archaeological evidence from Georgia shows wine being produced around 6000 BCE. Wine was first made by fermenting wild grapes, before humans began cultivating them. Through their empire, the Romans did much to spread knowledge of both grape cultivation and winemaking. Europe's vineyards suffered a terrible blow in the late nineteenth century, when a microscopic aphid called phylloxera was introduced from the United States and killed most of Europe's grapevines. The vineyards were saved by grafting European vines on to American ones, which were resistant to phylloxera. Today, grapes are grown in countries around the world, from the United Kingdom to New Zealand, and a remarkable variety of wines are made from their juice.

## MUSCAT GRAPE CRUSH

**Non-Alcoholic**
**(Serves 4–6)**

750g black muscat or Fragola grapes
50g soft brown sugar
50ml grape or sour cherry molasses
1 small lemon, juiced
Crushed ice
Soda water or sparkling water

When they are roasted, grapes turn sticky and their depth of flavour deepens. They make for a delicious non-alcoholic drink once crushed and topped with ice and soda water. Use a flavourful muscat or Fragola grape here if you can.

—

Heat the oven to 200°C/180°C fan. On a tray lined with parchment, toss the grapes together with the sugar and molasses. Roast in the oven for 30–35 minutes or until sticky and popping. Once roasted, leave to cool completely.

Pick the grapes off their stems and pop them into a high-speed blender, making sure to include all the sticky syrup from the tray. Blitz the grapes with the lemon juice, then spoon about 2 tbsp of the mixture into each glass. Top with crushed ice and soda water.

# WALNUT

***Juglans* species**

**The nuts of the wild walnut tree have been gathered and eaten for thousands of years. In Roman mythology, the walnut tree was associated with Jupiter, the ruler of all the gods; its Latin name is derived from *Jovis glans*, meaning "Jupiter's nut" or "Jupiter's acorn". A number of trees belong to the *Juglans* genus, including *J. regia*, also known as the English walnut, and they grow in the world's temperate regions. Fresh, new-season walnuts are a seasonal treat in many countries.**

Young green walnuts, while their shells are still soft, can be pickled – which turns them black – and eaten whole, usually enjoyed with cheese or charcuterie and also used to make walnut ketchup. As walnuts ripen, their shell hardens, protecting the edible kernels within. These kernels have a distinctive wrinkled shape, reflected in their expressive Afghan name, *charmaghz*, meaning "four brains".

Walnuts are a versatile ingredient for savoury and sweet dishes. In Liguria, Italy, they are ground to make a sauce for pasta. Finely ground walnuts are used to enrich and thicken sauces in recipes such as Circassian chicken, a historic dish also found in Turkey, and Persian *fesenjān*, which also boasts pomegranate molasses. Walnuts are key in Georgian cuisine, including as a filling for aubergine rolls or baked fish. In Greece and the Middle East, they are used as a nut filling, sandwiched between layers of filo pastry to make sweet, syrup-soaked baklava, while in Lebanon, they are used as a filling for small pastries called *ma'amoul*. France produces both walnut bread and walnut oil, which is used to dress salads rather than to cook, while in Britain, coffee and walnut cake remains a traditional tea-time favourite.

When it comes to drinks, green walnuts are used in Italy to make *nocino* liqueur, enjoyed straight or used in cocktails.

## WALNUT MARTINI

(Serves 1)

60ml gin or vodka
15ml dry vermouth
30ml walnut liqueur
Ice
Lemon twist, to serve

If you're already a lover of the Martini, why not try this nutty version made with sweet walnut liqueur? Stirred or shaken – it's your preference.

—

Stir or shake everything together with some ice in a cocktail shaker. Strain into a chilled martini glass and garnish with a twist of lemon.

# HOP

***Humulus lupulus***

**Although the young, tender shoots of wild hops are enjoyed as a vegetable in Europe, the climbing hop plant is primarily prized for its pale green female flower clusters, known as hop cones. These fragrant flowers have long been used to add to beer a flavour that is both distinctive and bitter.**

The earliest mention of hops used in brewing is in the ninth century in Germany. People noticed that hops had an important preservative function in brewing, as their presence inhibited the growth of bacteria that causes beer to spoil; this led to their cultivation and widespread use in beer-making.

Hops grow well in temperate northern zones. In Britain, the southern county of Kent has been especially associated with hop-growing for centuries. Oast houses, with their distinctive conical roofs, were originally built as places in which to dry hops for brewing and are a characteristic Kentish sight. Hop cones are ready to harvest in the autumn – during the nineteenth century, a tradition developed among London's East End working class of spending a few weeks in the Kentish countryside picking hops.

There are numerous hop varieties, each imparting specific notes to the beers they are used to make. Old World hops are known for their subtle, bitter flavours. One notable British hop variety was developed by Richard Fuggle, of Brenchley in Kent. Named after him, the Fuggle hop is regarded as a quintessential British hop, imparting a delicate minty and grassy flavour to beer. In contrast, what are called "New World hops", cultivated in North America, have a more pronounced tangy note, such as grapefruit. Craft brewers are innovating, blending hops to amalgamate diverse features in their products. The rise of these craft beers has also piqued the interest of mixologists, as they borrow the myriad elements of beer to fashion new and unusual cocktails.

## LAGERITA

**A lighter, longer version of a margarita. Great for those that want the usually short drink to last a little longer.**

—

**(Serves 2)**

**Tajin, for the rim of the glass (or make your own, page 110)**
**70ml tequila**
**30ml Cointreau**
**40ml lime juice**
**½ tsp agave syrup**
**Ice**
**Mexican beer**
**Slice of lime, to serve**

Chill two tall glasses. To add a spicy or simple salt rim to the glass, rub the rim of the chilled glasses with a lime wedge before dipping in Tajin or sea salt.

Add the tequila, Cointreau, lime juice and agave syrup to a cocktail shaker, top with ice and shake well.

Strain into the prepared glasses and top up each with roughly 150ml beer, and stir very gently. Serve with a slice of lime.

# APPLE

***Malus domestica***

**Widely cultivated and consumed, the apple is a fruit we hold dear – and one associated with many myths, legends and folk tales. In Greek mythology, golden apples grow on the tree of life in the Garden of Hesperides, while in Norse mythology, the gods eat apples which confer eternal youth.**

In Western art, the forbidden fruit that grows on the Tree of the Knowledge of Good and Evil in the Garden of Eden, and which is eaten by Adam and Eve, is depicted as an apple. It has an established reputation as a healthy fruit, as the old saying "An apple a day keeps the doctor away" suggests.

Over the centuries, hundreds of apple cultivars have been created, including both eating apples or desert apples, which can be eaten raw, and cooking apples, which are far more tart. Historically, Britain cultivated numerous apple varieties. The Bramley – first grown in the nineteenth century – is the UK's most popular cooking apple, characterized by its flesh that becomes fluffy when cooked. The apple is a versatile fruit in the kitchen, used in both sweet and savoury dishes. It is often paired with pork – as in roast pork with apple sauce – with the sweet-sour note a counterpoint to the fatty meat. Classic sweet apple-based treats include Britain's apple crumble, the Netherlands' apple cake and the apple pie of the United States.

Apples are also pressed for their juice. Depending on the varieties used, the flavour of the juice ranges from sweet to sharp. Since ancient times, apple juice has been fermented and turned into an alcoholic drink called cider. There are British heritage cider apple varieties, such as Foxwhelp and Yarlington Mill – too sour and tannic to be enjoyed as eating apples – which are specifically used for cider production. In Normandy, France, apple juice is turned into an apple brandy known as Calvados – both enjoyed on its own and in cocktails – while the United States produces applejack, made in a similar way to Calvados.

## MULLED APPLE

(Serves 4)

750ml good-quality apple juice
2 cinnamon sticks
2 star anise
3 cardamom pods, lightly bashed
Nutmeg, generous grating
150ml dark rum (optional)
Apple slices, to serve

An excellent tipple for warming the cockles on a crisp autumnal day. Try using a good-quality apple juice here – one made from a sharper apple, like russet or Cox, works well. This recipe is easy to double if you want to make it for a crowd, and it can easily be reheated.

—

Add the apple juice and all the aromatics to a pan and warm on a gentle simmer for 10 minutes. If using rum, add it and heat for another 5 minutes. Pour into heatproof glasses and serve with apple slices.

# JUNIPER

***Juniperus communis***

**A member of the evergreen cypress family, juniper is found in temperate northern regions, and ranges in size and form from a low-lying shrub to a small tree. For centuries, people have braved its spiky, needle-shaped leaves to collect the plant's female cones, known as juniper berries.**

With their distinctive pine fragrance and taste, they are an established and esteemed culinary spice. The Romans, according to Pliny the Elder, adulterated costly pepper with the small, round juniper berries. Juniper's aromatic pungency enhances meat and game, including sausages and pâtés. In Germany, it is added to their famous sauerkraut.

Juniper is best known for its use in alcoholic drinks, notably the clear spirit known as gin. Both the name "gin" and the drink itself can be traced back to a traditional Dutch spirit called genever. Genever, which is the Dutch word for juniper, is infused with herbs and spices, including juniper berries. Having acquired a taste for Holland's genever, Britain developed gin – and, following the accession of William of Orange to the throne in 1689, gin became hugely popular in Britain. The loosening of licensing laws led to an explosive boom in gin production and consumption during the first half of the eighteenth century. Concerns over the social consequences of excessive gin-drinking saw the British government restricting its production and sale.

A style of gin known as London dry gin, in which the zip of juniper is prominent, developed. During the nineteenth century, the British in India paired gin with quinine-based tonic (since quinine was known to combat malaria), creating that classic cocktail, the G & T. The relaxation in 2008 of laws restricting gin production resulted in a rise of craft distilleries across Britain, estimated to number 820 in 2022. Today's gin distillers have broadened their offerings to incorporate botanicals like watercress, chilli or peppercorns, but in order to be classified as gin, the spirit must contain juniper.

## JUNIPER GIN FIZZ

(Serves 1)

3 dried juniper berries, plus extra to serve
1 star anise
50ml dry gin
1 tbsp lemon juice
½ tbsp sugar syrup
Ice
Soda water
Slice of grapefruit, to serve

If you like the rich botanical flavour of gin, this is a great way to enhance it. Adding some extra toasted juniper and a star anise gives you that real hit of fragrant spicing.

—

In a dry frying pan, toast the juniper and star anise over a medium heat for 5 minutes. Tip them into a cocktail shaker with the gin, lemon juice and sugar syrup and shake together.

Strain into a tall glass, topping with ice and soda water. Garnish with grapefruit and a couple of juniper berries.

# TURMERIC

***Curcuma longa***

**The turmeric plant is indigenous to India, and its small, slender rhizomes have been grown and used as both a dye and a spice for thousands of years. Indeed, it has been cultivated for so long that it no longer exists in its wild state, and requires human propagation.**

Peeling or cutting a piece of fresh turmeric reveals an inside that is bright orange. Thanks to the presence of the chemical curcumin, turmeric has a great capacity to stain cloth yellow, hence its historic importance as a dye. It is also used in Ayurvedic medicine and traditional Chinese medicine, where it is prescribed for its many properties, including improving digestion.

A member of the ginger family, turmeric has a warm, gingery aroma when fresh. It is consumed both in this form and, more commonly, in its dried, powdered form. It is frequently included in curry powders and pastes and is also a key spice in North Africa's ras-al-hanout spice blend. Turmeric adds colour and spice to numerous dishes in Indian cuisine, from dals and curries to chutneys and pickles. Turmeric is also widely used in Southeast Asia – for example, in Malaysia's *nasi kunyit* (a celebratory dish of yellow stained rice), in Thai curry pastes, Vietnamese fish dishes and in Singapore's laksa (fish noodle soup). In the West, turmeric is found in curry powders, adding a distinctive touch of yellow to recipes such as coronation chicken or kedgeree.

Thanks to its anti-inflammatory reputation, fresh turmeric is more widely available in the UK than it used to be: shots of recently squeezed juice are sold in health food stores and supermarkets, and turmeric is added to smoothies. Golden-coloured turmeric chai latte is enjoying a moment too.

## TURMERIC GOLD RUSH

**(Serves 1)**

Ice
60ml bourbon
1 tsp fresh turmeric, finely grated
1 tbsp lemon juice
2–3 tbsp runny honey (to your personal taste)
Small pinch of salt
50ml water
Lemon twist, to serve

This cocktail packs a punch: fresh turmeric's notes of pepper and ginger, and the sweetness of honey. Serve over ice in a chilled glass.

—

Fill a tumbler with ice and chill.

In a cocktail shaker, add the bourbon, turmeric, lemon juice, honey, salt and water. Shake vigorously, then strain into the glass with a twist of lemon.

# ROSE HIP

***Rosa* species**

**Bright scarlet or orange-red when ripe, the rose hip, the name given to the small, glossy "fruit" of the rose, is valued as an ingredient in its own right, quite separately from the fragrant flower. Botanically speaking, the rose hip is what is called a "false fruit": the real fruit is contained within it.**

For centuries, people have foraged the rose hips of the wild dog rose (*Rosa canina*) from hedgerows, braving the plant's sharp thorns for the precious fruit, which were widely used in traditional medicine. The seventeenth-century English herbalist Nicholas Culpeper valued rose hips for their "restorative" effects, advising that they be used to treat "consumptive persons" and coughs. In more recent times, rose hips have been valued for their high vitamin C content, which is around 20 times higher than that of oranges, and their iron content. In Britain during the Second World War, schoolchildren and scout troops were sent into the countryside to pick rose hips as a patriotic duty, so that National Rose Hip Syrup could be made and given as a dietary supplement to small children.

Rather than eaten raw, rose hips, which have a distinctive tartness with no fragrant rose notes, are cooked, usually in recipes that feature sugar or some other sweetener. The English herbalist Gerard (1545–1612) wrote of them: "The fruit when it is ripe maketh the most pleasant meats and banqueting dishes as tarts and such-like; the making of which I commit to the cunning cook." Traditional country recipes for rose hips include turning them into preserves such as rose hip jelly, rose hip jam, rose hip and apple "cheese" (a sweet, dense fruit paste, like *membrillo*) and rose hip vinegar. Rose hip wine is another rural recipe that makes the most of this seasonal fruit. As in wartime, rose hip syrup remains a popular way of cooking rose hips, and rose hip syrup adds both a beautiful taste and a coral red colour to cocktails.

# ROSE HIP SYRUP

**Make a batch of sweet rose hip syrup in the chillier autumn months. It's delicious drunk as it is with fizzy water, lemon and ice, or added to a G & T.**

—

**MAKES 1 LITRE**

**1kg rose hips, thoroughly washed**
**1.25 litres cold water**
**About 500g golden caster sugar**

Remove the stems from the rose hips and discard. Roughly chop the rose hips and add them to your largest pan along with 1.25 litres of cold water. Bring to a simmer, and once there, set a timer for 20 minutes.

After this time, strain the mixture into a large saucepan through a sieve lined with muslin. Leave the strainer to sit for 1 hour to get as much of the liquid as you can. Measure your juice – for every 500ml, you need roughly 350g sugar. Add the sugar to the juice and simmer for 15 minutes, stirring until the sugar has dissolved. Raise the heat and boil for 5 minutes, then skim off any scum from the surface.

While the liquid is hot, decant it into sterilized jars or glass bottles. Leave these to cool completely – the syrup will last for six months in a cool, dry place. Once opened, store in the fridge for four weeks.

Add the syrup to a G & T, have it in a spritz with sparkling wine, or enjoy it diluted with water, ice and a squeeze of lemon juice.

# PEAR

***Pyrus communis***

**Like the apple, the pear originated in the Caucasus region. From the original wild pear tree, there are now hundreds of cultivated varieties. Pears were grown by the Greeks and Romans, who ate the fruit both raw and cooked.**

One of the distinctions made among European pear varieties is between those with a firmer flesh that retains its shape when cooked, such as Conference, and soft-fleshed eating pears, such as the smooth-textured Doyenné du Comice.

The simple pleasures of perfectly ripe, juicy pears are considerable. The French enjoy cooking them with game birds and animals, such as duck and hare, and they go well with blue cheese in salads or canapés. More usually, pears are cooked in sweet dishes: fruit tarts, refreshing sorbets, compotes and conserves. Poaching whole pears in red wine flavoured with spices is a textbook way of serving them, and one which makes the most of their distinctive and appealing shape. Another well-known dessert is Pears Belle Helene, created by the famous French chef Escoffier, in which pears poached in a vanilla syrup are paired with vanilla ice cream and chocolate sauce, a delightful combination.

Among the many varieties are a number of astringent pears – Barnet, Blakeney Red, Stinking Bishop – used for making perry, the pear equivalent of cider, made from fermented pear juice. In Britain, the production of perry is particularly associated with the counties of Gloucestershire, Herefordshire and Worcestershire. Although it's not widely produced, some small-scale producers maintain the perry tradition, offering both still and sparkling options. Poire Williams – made from Williams or Bartlett pears – is a sweet liqueur often served chilled as an after-dinner drink or as an ingredient in cocktails, such as a perini or pear brandy Old Fashioned.

# PEAR AND VANILLA DAIQUIRI

(Serves 1)

2 pears, peeled and cored
1 vanilla pod, seeds scraped out
3 tbsp caster sugar
½ lemon, juice only, plus 25ml lemon juice
Lots of ice
50ml white rum

**Pear and vanilla are cooked into a sweet puree before being added to this classic white-rum cocktail.**

**Use a good-quality vanilla pod if possible.**

—

Tip the pears into a saucepan with the vanilla pod and seeds, sugar, juice of half a lemon and 2 tbsp water. Simmer for 12–15 minutes, covered, until the pears have broken down into a thick puree. Strain through a sieve and allow to cool.

Spoon 3 tbsp of the cooled puree into a cocktail shaker with lots of ice, the rum and 25ml lemon juice. Shake well and strain into a glass.

Use the remaining puree to make more cocktails or spoon it into flutes and top with sparkling wine, like crémant.

# LAVENDER

***Lavandula angustifolia***

**Indigenous to the western Mediterranean, the lavender plant – with its slender silvery leaves and spikes of small purple flowers – is much loved by gardeners and a familiar sight in parks and gardens. An intensely fragrant plant, it has been lauded for centuries for its aromatic and medicinal properties.**

It was even mentioned in the Bible as one of the holy herbs used in Solomon's Temple. For millennia, lavender oil has been used to add aroma to perfumes, soaps and detergents. It is a key component of potpourri mixtures, designed to be placed in wardrobes to scent clothing. Its fragrance is thought to be calming and conducive to sleep, so lavender pillows are popular.

Because it is strong, lavender is used judiciously in the kitchen. It is one of the herbs in France's *herbes de Provence* mixture, employed for grilled fish and meat, and is sometimes used to flavour cheese, such as soft goat's or sheep's milk cheeses. It is also used in sweet baking, adding its celebrated characteristics to shortbread biscuits, dainty cupcakes, brownies and rich, smooth-textured crème brulée – and lavender flowers serve as the perfect decorative garnish. It lends itself well to chocolate, so is often found in bars, truffles and desserts like mousse. Lavender sugar can easily be made at home by placing sprigs of the plant in a jar of caster sugar to infuse for several weeks. Lavender is beloved by bees and lavender honey, made with nectar sourced from lavender flowers, is appreciated for its delicate floral notes, which pair beautifully with goat's cheese.

Lavender syrup is a hit with bartenders, but it is often mixed into drinks alongside other fragrant herbs. For example, it is one of the ingredients in vermouths, the family of lightly fortified wines that are heavily aromatized with herbs and spices. Makers of craft gin, too, call on it as a botanical addition to their spirits.

# HONEY AND LAVENDER WHISKY SOUR

Don't be put off by the strong flavour of lavender. Once infused into this cocktail, it adds a lovely sweetness with a gentle hum of honey.

—

**FOR THE LAVENDER SYRUP**

100ml water
100g runny blossom honey
5 tbsp dried lavender buds

—

**FOR THE COCKTAIL (Serves 1)**

2 tbsp lavender syrup
50ml bourbon
1 medium egg white
35ml lemon juice
Ice cubes
A sprig of lavender, to serve

Tip the water, honey and lavender into a saucepan, then simmer gently for 10 minutes or until a little reduced and syrupy. Strain into a clean jar and leave to cool completely. Keep the syrup in a sealed jar in the fridge for up to one month.

Place 2 tbsp of the lavender syrup in a cocktail shaker with bourbon, egg white, lemon juice and ice cubes. Shake vigorously and strain into a chilled tumbler filled with lots of ice. Garnish with a sprig of lavender.

# TAMARIND

***Tamarindus indica***

**Native to Madagascar, the tamarind tree reached India so long ago that it was assumed to be indigenous to India. The tree bears its fruit in brown pods and this fruit is both eaten fresh and used as a spice in a number of cuisines, including Indian, Mexican and Southeast Asian. While it doesn't possess much odour, tamarind has a distinctive sour-sweet taste due to the presence of tartaric acid, alongside natural sugars in the pulp.**

From a culinary perspective, tamarind is used to add a pleasing sourness to many dishes, in the same way that lemon juice is. In the kitchen, it's normally in the form of tamarind paste or water. Both of these are made from the dried sticky pulp of the tamarind fruit. A portion of the pulp is soaked in water for several minutes, then strained to remove any seeds and fibrous parts, resulting in either tamarind paste or water, depending on how much water was used.

In the tropics, it is often seen in seafood dishes, providing a subtle tang. Traditionally, tamarind was believed to have antibacterial properties and research has discovered that this is indeed the case, which makes its use practical as well as delicious. In Indian cuisine, tamarind is added to numerous dishes: curries, vegetable and pulse dishes and condiments. Date and tamarind sauce is a key component of dishes such as chickpea chaat. In Malaysia, sambal prawns are a spicy dish cooked with chilli, shrimp paste and tamarind. In Britain, tamarind is a familiar presence in kitchen cupboards – albeit in the disguised form of Worcestershire sauce or brown sauce. In a number of tropical countries, tamarind is used to create refreshing drinks, such as Mexico's *agua de tamarindo* (tamarind water).

## TAMARIND WHISKY SOUR

(Serves 1)

50ml bourbon
½ tsp tamarind paste
30ml lime juice
1–2 tbsp sugar syrup
½ egg white
Ice, including 1 large cube

**Sharp tamarind's rich, savoury flavour works well in this cocktail alongside a good smoky bourbon.**

—

Tip the bourbon, tamarind paste, lime juice, sugar syrup and egg white into a cocktail shaker with a good handful of ice and shake vigorously.

Strain into a chilled rocks glass with a large ice cube.

# WINTER

# BAY

***Laurus nobilis***

**As its Latin name suggests, the bay or laurel has long been a prestigious herb. A Greek myth relates how a beautiful nymph being hotly pursued by an amorous Apollo, God of music, begged her river-god father to help her, so he transformed her into a laurel tree.**

Thereafter, the laurel was considered sacred to Apollo, with the god often depicted wearing a laurel wreath. In ancient Greece, the fragrant, glossy, dark green leaves of this evergreen shrub or small tree – native to the Mediterranean region – were woven into garlands and used to crown kings, victorious generals, poets and successful athletes. The Romans maintained the tradition of bestowing laurel wreaths on Olympic athletes and emperors as a mark of honour. During the Renaissance period, students receiving a doctorate were awarded a branch of laurel bearing berries, hence the term “baccalaureate” (meaning “berried laurel” in Latin), which is still used today.

Aromatic bay leaves are also an important culinary herb, usually used whole, either fresh or dried. A bay leaf is a key component of France’s *bouquet garni*, a small bunch of herbs used to season sauces and stews, such as beef daubes, court bouillon (a spiced liquid used for poaching fish, shellfish or chicken) and slow-simmered homemade chicken or meat stock. A whole bay leaf is traditionally laid on top of a pâté or terrine before it is baked to perfume the meat and is often used to infuse hot milk for a béchamel sauce. Bay leaves are also incorporated in sweet dishes, such as rice pudding or poached fruit compotes, and add an intriguing note to custard.

When it comes to tipples, in Italy, bay leaves are used with a spirit such as vodka to create a liqueur called *allorino* – *alloro* is Italian for a bay tree or laurel. This can be sipped neat or mixed with Prosecco to make a bay-infused spritz.

## BAY NEGRONI

Fresh bay leaves are infused into this festive drink, along with a whole host of spiced aromatics. If you're a fan of a classic Negroni, you will love this wintry version.

—

(Serves 4)

2 cinnamon sticks
4 whole cloves
2 star anise
2 cardamom pods, crushed
1 tsp peppercorns
3 fresh bay leaves
200ml gin
Ice
100–200ml vermouth
100–200ml Campari
Orange slices and fresh bay leaves, to serve

Put the cinnamon, cloves, star anise, cardamom and peppercorns in a dry frying pan and toast for 5 minutes, or until the spices are just fragrant. Remove from the heat and leave to cool.

Tip all the toasted spices into a medium jar, add the bay leaves and pour the gin in on top. Seal and chill for 48 hours to infuse.

Strain the infused gin through a fine mesh sieve, and fill four to eight glasses with ice. To mix the cocktail, tip 25ml each of infused gin, vermouth and Campari into the glasses, then garnish with orange slices and bay leaves. Any leftover infused gin will keep, sealed in a cool, dry place, for up to two months.

# CLOVE

***Syzygium aromaticum***

**The history of cloves – the small, dried, unopened buds of the evergreen clove tree – gives an insight into just how valuable spices were for centuries.**

Cloves are native to Indonesia's Molucca Islands – which, with their valuable trees, were hotly disputed by European colonial powers and taken first by the Portuguese, then the Dutch, who created a monopoly in the early seventeenth century by destroying most of the clove trees so they could control supply. The French broke the Dutch monopoly by introducing clove seedlings to Réunion and Madagascar. Today, cloves are grown in tropical countries, and Indonesia is the largest producer.

The shape of cloves do resemble nails – and the name "clove" derives from the French name *clou de girofle*, meaning "nail of clove". Their nail-like shape and hardness explains why one traditional use of cloves in Europe is to stud oranges to create fragrant pomanders to scent drawers. Cloves have a powerful odour and flavour, with eugenol the main flavour component. Eugenol is a natural anaesthetic and clove oil has long been used to treat toothache. Another non-culinary use is in Indonesia's *kretek* cigarettes, the main reason for Indonesia growing cloves on so large a scale.

Due to their penetrating smell and taste, cloves are often used with discretion in the kitchen. For example, a peeled onion studded with a few cloves is a traditional flavouring for a British bread sauce, while one or two cloves might be used with other seasonings to perfume a basmati rice pilaf or to spice pickled pears. Roast ham dotted with cloves sees them used more generously, as the aroma compliments the sumptuousness of the meat. Cloves are frequently found in seasoning blends, such as China's five-spice powder, India's curry powders and France's *quatre-épices* ("four spices"). They are often added to drinks such as mulled wine or cider, while clove-infused syrups are deployed in cocktails.

## SPICED OLD FASHIONED

(Serves 1)

150ml water
150ml brown sugar
6 cloves
3 Sichuan peppercorns
1 dash angostura bitters
60ml bourbon
Soda water
Twist of orange peel, to serve

**Up your Old Fashioned game by adding a few spices from your store cupboard for a comforting, toasty hit.**

—

Tip the water, sugar, cloves and peppercorns into a pan. Bring to a simmer and cook for 5 minutes. Strain into a jar and leave to cool. The syrup will keep in a sealed jar in the fridge for up to one month.

Put 2 tbsp spiced syrup into a glass. Add a splash of water, the bitters and bourbon and then top up with soda. Finish with a twist of orange peel.

# GINGER

***Zingiber officinale***

**Ginger, the rhizome (underground stem) of the ginger plant, has a venerable history of culinary usage. It has been an important spice for thousands of years, central to several Asian cuisines, among them Chinese, Indian and Southeast Asian.**

Indeed, ginger has been cultivated by humans for so many centuries that the plant can now only be grown by splitting the root – not grown from seed. The wild ancestor of ginger has not been traced, but it originated either in northeastern India or southern China. Sought after for its health properties, it was regarded by the ancient Greeks as an antidote to poison. In a number of societies, it is believed to help with digestive problems.

The distinctive pungency of the rhizome is thanks to the presence of gingerols, phytochemical compounds created by the plant. It is a noticeably versatile spice, one that is used in both fresh and preserved forms (dried, candied or pickled) for savoury and sweet items. In Chinese cooking, fresh ginger is prized for its capacity to neutralize fishy or meaty aromas in dishes such as steamed sea bass, and is often paired with spring onion. In Japanese cuisine, thin slices of pickled ginger are served as a palate cleanser alongside sushi or sashimi. In the Indian kitchen, it is mixed with garlic, onions and aromatic spices to create a range of curries. Ginger was a crowd-pleaser in medieval Europe, famously used to make gingerbread, which for centuries was a popular fairground treat. In the Europe of today, ground ginger finds its way into biscuits and cakes.

Ginger's powerful taste has also made it a nearly ubiquitous ingredient in both alcoholic and non-alcoholic beverages, ranging from ginger wines and cordials to tea and kombucha. Included in these is ginger beer, which can be found in both low-alcohol and alcohol-free versions. Historically, this was made by fermenting a mixture of sugar, ginger, water, lemons and cream of tartar. Nowadays, ginger beer is widely produced using carbon dioxide to create its characteristic bubbles.

# GINGER AND HONEY SWITCHEL

**Non-Alcoholic (Serves 4–6)**

200g fresh root ginger, peeled and sliced

150g soft light brown sugar

50g raw runny honey

100ml raw cider vinegar

1 litre boiling water

Ice

The switchel originated in the Caribbean, and is not so different from kombucha. I like to think of it as a lighter, beginners' drinking vinegar. It is still rather than fizzy, and a little sweeter than kombucha. You can drink this straight over ice or dilute it: two-thirds switchel to one-third fizzy water. It's great if you're laying off the booze, as its sharp, zingy flavour tricks you into thinking you're sipping on something stronger.

—

Place the ginger in a 1.5-litre sterilized jar. Add the brown sugar, honey and vinegar, then pour the boiling water in. Leave to cool at room temperature, then seal and chill in the fridge for 24 hours (and up to three days).

Strain over a glass filled with ice and drink it as it is, or top up with sparkling water.

0.75

# LIQUORICE

***Glycyrrhiza* species**

**There is a divisive quality to liquorice – people either love it or loathe it! It is made from the dried rhizomes of the liquorice plant (*Glycyrrhiza* species). It grows in different regions of the world and has been cultivated in both Europe and China for several centuries, and is appreciated for its medicinal properties, including the capacity to alleviate coughs and aid digestion.**

The Chinese name for the plant means "sweet herb" – it contains a compound called glycyrrhizin that is 50 times sweeter than sugar. This natural sweetness has meant that liquorice rhizomes (often called liquorice root) has a venerable history of being used to make confectionery. Yorkshire was a centre of liquorice production in Britain, and the town of Pontefract became famous in the seventeenth century for its coin-shaped liquorice sweets, known as Pontefract cakes, made originally in a local monastery. Liquorice's capacity to be shaped has resulted in ingenious confectionery – among them long, thin liquorice "shoelaces" and Britain's liquorice allsorts, in which liquorice is combined with sugar paste and coconut to create a colourful mixture of sweets in assorted shapes. The Dutch and the Scandinavians have a fondness for liquorice in many forms: sweet and salty, soft and hard versions, produced in an array of shapes, such as little cats, stars and bears. Liquorice ice cream is also enjoying a moment. In Chinese cuisine, it is one of the components of five-spice powder.

Liquorice water, made by infusing the rhizomes in water, is a traditional drink, appreciated for its refreshing qualities. In the Middle East, it is enjoyed during Ramadan, the Islamic period of fasting. Liquorice is also used as an ingredient in America's root beer, a beverage initially drunk for health reasons, but which evolved into a popular soft drink enjoyed for its distinctive flavour.

## LIQUORICE AND BLACKCURRANT COCKTAIL

Aniseed-rich liquorice and sweet blackcurrants make for a fantastic combination along with a hit of booze. Drink as it is, or top up with soda water to dilute.

—

(Serves 1)

½ tbsp liquorice syrup
50ml crème de cassis
25ml vodka or gin
Ice
Soda water to taste

Tip the liquorice syrup, crème de cassis and vodka or gin into a cocktail shaker with a handful of ice. Shake well.

Serve over ice in tumblers.

# CINNAMON

***Cinnamomum verum***

**Long valued and traded as a precious spice, cinnamon is made from the bark of the cinnamon tree, which is indigenous to Sri Lanka. A historic confusion between what is sometimes called "true cinnamon" and cassia, produced from the bark of the closely related cassia tree (*Cinnamomum aromaticum*), persists to this day.**

Fantastic tales about cinnamon's origins include a story told by the ancient Greek historian Herodotus, suggesting that cinnamon sticks were used as nesting material by large birds in the Arabian mountains.

In the process of gathering and producing cinnamon, the inner bark of the cinnamon tree is periodically stripped, scraped, folded, dried and rolled, producing slender rolls known as cinnamon quills. With its warm, sweet fragrance, cinnamon is central to many dishes in both its quill form and as a finely ground powder. In Indian cooking, it is used in fragrant spice mixtures such as garam masala and in dishes including pilafs. In the Moroccan kitchen, cinnamon adds fragrance to tagines and to *bastille*, a luxurious pie made with spiced pigeon. Cinnamon has a well-known affinity with apples, so is a classic ingredient for dishes such as American apple pie or British apple crumble. In Portugal's irresistible *pasteis de nata* (custard tarts), the custard is traditionally made with cinnamon and lemon, then sprinkled with ground cinnamon and icing sugar.

Cinnamon also plays a role in various drinks. It blends beautifully with both chocolate and coffee; a sprinkling of powdered cinnamon is sometimes added to hot chocolate or milky drinks like lattes as a finishing touch. It is also a favourite for tea drinkers, as one of the spices classically used in chai, India's aromatic spiced tea. In the cold winter months, cinnamon comes into its own as an addition for warming tipples such as mulled wine and cider or Swedish *glögg*. As well as being used to infuse syrups, cinnamon sticks are a standard decorative garnish for cocktails.

## HOT TODDY

(Serves 1)

50ml bourbon
120ml boiling water
2 tbsp blossom honey
1 large cinnamon stick
3 cloves
50ml lemon juice, plus a slice to serve

**Warm yourself up in the colder months with this seasonal cocktail warmly spiced with cinnamon and cloves. Make sure you use a fresh cinnamon stick – any that have been sitting dormant on your spice rack may have lost their heady fragrance.**

—

Pour the bourbon, boiling water, honey, cinnamon and cloves into a mug. Leave this to steep for 5 minutes, remove the cloves, then stir in the lemon juice and garnish with the lemon slice.

# ROSEMARY

***Salvia rosmarinus***

**Regarded as a quintessentially Mediterranean herb, the rosemary plant is indeed indigenous to the region. While it can grow in cooler environs, it thrives in warm, sunny climes. It is a woody, evergreen perennial shrub featuring narrow leaves that are dark green above and pale beneath, and small flowers that are usually purple or blue.**

It is a herb rich in legend and folklore. The colour of the flowers is attributed to the Virgin Mary throwing her cloak on a bush when she rested during her flight to Egypt. It was viewed as a plant that protects against witchcraft and the evil eye. It had a reputation for strengthening memory and so was a symbol of fidelity; hence Ophelia's line "There's rosemary, that's for remembrance" in *Hamlet*. Thanks to its association with faithfulness, rosemary wreaths were historically worn by brides, while branches of rosemary, decorated with silk ribbons, were given to wedding guests.

The plant has a pronounced scent with notes of pine and camphor. A traditional culinary use for rosemary leaves is in marinades, and whole sprigs of it are added to stews. In France, it is one of the herbs that make up the *herbes de Provence* mix. In Italian cooking, rosemary is added to roast potatoes, bean soups and focaccia.

When it comes to drinks, rosemary – with its powerful aroma and taste and perceived health-giving properties – was regarded as a "cordial herb" in medieval times, and used to flavour ale and wines. Rosemary tea, made by steeping a sprig in hot water, is a simple tisane. Rosemary oil, extracted through distillation, is used by the drinks industry. Gin makers use rosemary in combination with other fragrant ingredients, while rosemary-infused syrups, vinegars and honey are de rigueur with bartenders.

## ROSEMARY BRAMBLE

**(Serves 1)**

50ml gin
1 sprig of rosemary, pines stripped, plus extra to serve
25 ml lemon juice
1 tbsp sugar syrup
Ice
25 ml crème de mûre
Fresh blackberries, to serve

**This is the drink to make when the hedgerows are growing ripe with fat blackberries. The fragrant rosemary is delicious with the sweet fruit, making this an impeccable choice for a post-forage tipple.**

—

Tip the gin into a cocktail shaker, add the rosemary, lemon juice and sugar syrup and some ice and shake well. Strain into a glass filled with crushed ice. Trickle over the crème du mûre so it "bleeds" into the ice.

Finish with a sprig of rosemary and some fresh blackberries.

# NUTMEG

***Myristica fragrans***

**Native to Indonesia, nutmeg was once so highly prized that the Banda Islands where it grew were fought over and possessed by colonial powers including the Portuguese, Dutch, French and British for centuries.**

The nutmeg tree, in fact, produces two spices: mace (the netlike aril around the seed) and nutmeg, the nut or seed. So rare and costly was nutmeg that by 1760, the price of a pound of nutmeg in London was more than 80 shillings (more than £400 today). Nowadays, nutmeg is grown in a number of tropical countries, and the Caribbean island of Grenada is renowned for it.

Nutmeg's distinctive, warm, rich aroma and flavour is best released by grating it – particularly as a finishing touch for foods like pumpkin soup, mashed potato or rice pudding. Special, small, fine-toothed graters (some with a little compartment in which to store a whole nutmeg) have long been produced specifically for this purpose, although the spice is also sold ready-ground.

It adds its aromatic fragrance to curries, France's béchamel sauce and *quatre-épices* spice blend and the fillings for Italian stuffed pasta and spinach dishes. One of the spices in gingerbread, it features on the recipe cards for rich fruit cakes and Indonesia's *kue lapis*, a multilayered spice cake also known as *spekkoek* (which means "bacon cake", because of its layered appearance, in Dutch).

A sprinkling of freshly grated nutmeg can be an important finishing touch for drinks such as mulled wine, cider or punch. During the eighteenth century, when this spice was an exotic luxury, silver nutmeg graters were a status symbol among the wealthy elite. Today, in the United States, the Christmas drink of eggnog is topped with a touch of freshly grated nutmeg or ground cinnamon, while the luxurious, creamy cocktail known as a Brandy Alexander is served sprinkled with grated or ground nutmeg.

## NUTMEG ALEXANDER

**(Serves 1)**

50ml brandy
30ml crème de cacao
30ml double cream
Ice
Nutmeg, freshly grated

A decadent dessert cocktail. An Alexander was originally made with gin, but this brandy version works beautifully with nutmeg. Crème de cacao comes in both clear and dark varieties – either will work here. You could also add a small sprinkle of cinnamon powder along with the dusting of nutmeg.

—

Add the brandy, crème de cacao, cream and a generous amount of ice to a shaker. Shake well before straining into a chilled small cocktail glass. Freshly grate a dusting of nutmeg over the top.

# CARDAMOM

***Elettaria cardamomum***

**Sometimes called the "queen of spices", cardamom possesses a notable and distinctive fragrance. The cardamom plant, a broad-leafed, perennial herb, is indigenous to India and Sri Lanka.**

The small, dried fruits of the plant – light green in colour, sometimes bleached white – are known as cardamom pods. Inside these pods are dark brown seeds – which, if they are still dark and sticky, is a sign of freshness. Both the pods and the ground seeds are used to flavour food and drink. Historically, cardamom was traded as a valued spice and used in perfumes as well as in a culinary capacity. In traditional medicine in various countries, it is used to treat chest problems and as a breath freshener.

Cardamom's applications in the kitchen are numerous and diverse. In Indian cookery, it perfumes curries, including kormas, marinades and luxurious basmati rice dishes, including biriyanis. It is a vital flavouring for a variety of traditional Indian sweets, such as *barfi* (which resembles fudge), *kheer* (rice pudding) and *kulfi* (ice cream). Cardamom features in a number of spice mixtures, including the Middle East's *bahārāt* and Ethiopia's *berbere*. The Vikings introduced cardamom – after finding it in the bazaars of Constantinople – to their native Scandinavia, where it became a beloved spice in baking. It lends its complex, versatile taste to a huge range of pastries, biscuits and cakes, among them cardamom buns and cinnamon buns, two iconic snacks often enjoyed during *fika*, Sweden's coffee break. It is among the spices traditionally used for gingerbread.

Cardamom is also an important spice in the world of drinks. In the Middle East, people have added cardamom to their coffee for generations. In Scandinavia, cardamom pods are among the spices added to mulled wine, and it is a well-known botanical ingredient in gins worldwide.

## CARDAMOM ESPRESSO MARTINI

**(Serves 1)**

50ml vodka
25ml coffee liqueur
25ml espresso, cooled
2 cardamom pods, bashed, and seeds removed (husks discarded), plus some whole ones, to serve
Ice

This Espresso Martini takes inspiration from Turkish coffee. Heady cardamom offsets the rich coffee flavour and makes for a deliciously moreish cocktail.

—

Pour everything into a cocktail shaker with a handful of ice and shake vigorously for at least 1 minute. Strain into a chilled martini glass. Garnish with a couple of coffee beans or cardamom pods.

# PEPPER

***Piper nigrum***

**Alongside salt, with which it is overwhelmingly paired, pepper is a familiar, everyday spice in numerous households. It is so commonly used that it is usually stored in a pepper pot or grinder so as to be readily available. Historically, pepper was of paramount importance, playing a central role in the spice trade. It was greatly esteemed by the Romans: emperors regarded it as a form of currency and kept quantities of it in the treasury.**

Pepper is obtained from the tiny fruits, known as peppercorns, of a climbing vine. The plant is indigenous to South India, where the Malabar region is still noted for the quality of its pepper. Black pepper, the best-known form, is produced by picking the fruit when it is still slightly unripe, fermenting and then drying it; sun-drying is regarded as the best method. Green peppercorns are the unripe fruit and can be preserved by freezing, drying, canning or pickling in brine or vinegar. White pepper is created by picking the fruit when it is ripe, discarding the fleshy part and drying the white seed within. Red or pink peppercorns are the fully ripe fruit, usually preserved in brine or vinegar. Pepper has a characteristic, nose-tickling "spicy" taste and aroma, due to the presence of piperine.

Many dishes are seasoned with a touch of pepper as a matter of course. Peppercorns are often used in charcuterie products and cheeses. French cuisine has pepper take a prominent role in the dish *steak au poivre* (steak with pepper), as it is crushed into a creamy sauce that generously covers the meat. In Thailand, fresh green peppercorns are readily available in the markets and popped into stir-fries, curries and relishes. In India, pepper is used in a piquant soup called *rasam*, or pepper water. In European cookery, finely ground black pepper is traditionally used in gingerbread spice mixes. Pepper-infused syrups are designed to add an intriguing kick to cocktails.

## MICHELADA

**(Serves 1)**

**2 large ripe tomatoes**
**Lime wedge**
**Smoked salt or Tajin**
**Ice**
**30ml tequila (optional)**
**2–3 dashes Tabasco or other hot sauce**
**10ml lime juice**
**½ tsp ground black pepper**
**Mexican beer, to top up**
**Slice of lemon, to serve**

**A Michelada is a tomato-based cocktail – topped up with tequila, beer and a dash of hot sauce – that was first created in Mexico.**

—

Grate the tomatoes using a box grater, collecting the juice and discarding the skin and pips. You want to make 100ml juice, so you may need more tomatoes depending on how ripe and juicy they are. Strain through a fine sieve.

Rub the rim of a tall chilled glass with a lime wedge before dipping in the smoked salt or Tajin. Fill the glass a third of the way up with ice. Pour over the tomato juice, tequila, Tabasco, lime juice and pepper. Finally, top it up with beer and serve with a slice of lemon.

# HORSERADISH

***Armoracia rusticana***

**While the thick, fleshy roots of the horseradish plant resemble parsnips, its powerful smell and taste mean that it is used as a condiment rather than eaten as a vegetable.**

The horseradish root contains mustard oils, and when the root is broken through grating or grinding, a chemical reaction occurs that creates allyl isothiocyanate, a compound that triggers the "burning" sensation that causes eyes to water and noses to run. This compound is volatile, so quickly dissipates – and also loses its pungency when cooked.

The horseradish plant is indigenous to Eastern Europe and Western Asia and, like mustard, is treasured for its capacity to enliven food. It is exceedingly popular in Central Europe, where it is known as German mustard. It plays a prominent role in Jewish cuisine; it is one of the "five bitter herbs" traditionally eaten during Passover for the ritual meal known as the Seder. One popular way of using horseradish is grating it and mixing it with vinegar, salt and cream (or sour cream) to make horseradish sauce. The British town of Tewkesbury, in Gloucestershire, was noted for its Tewkesbury mustard, made by pounding together equal parts of mustard seed and horseradish and mentioned by the character Falstaff in William Shakespeare's play *Henry IV, Part 2*. The charismatic nineteenth-century chef Alexis Soyer used horseradish as one of the ingredients in his expressively named "Universal Devil's Mixture", a fiery marinade for meat that also featured chillies. In Britain, horseradish sauce, either freshly made or shop-bought, is a typical accompaniment to roast beef, while in Germany, it is often served with tongue. The sauce also goes well with beetroot, herring, ham, sausages and apples.

When it comes to cocktails, horseradish is a much-loved addition to the famous Bloody Mary, added alongside Tabasco sauce to give a fiery kick. Bartenders use it to add a mustard-y hit to drinks like Dirty Martinis or Margaritas, and to infuse vodka.

## HORSERADISH TOMATINI

The Tomatini is one of those modern cocktails that is set to be a classic. Use your best ripe tomatoes if you can. The addition of hot and peppery horseradish makes this savoury cocktail pack a punch.

—

(Serves 2)

2 large ripe tomatoes (use a winter variety if you're making this from October to December)
Large handful ice
120ml vodka
2 tbsp dry vermouth
¼ tsp sugar
1 tsp freshly grated horseradish
3 tbsp olive brine
Cherry tomatoes and olives, to serve

Chill two martini glasses in the freezer.

Using the coarse side of a box grater, grate the tomatoes into a bowl.

Combine ice, the tomato pulp and juice, vodka, vermouth, sugar, horseradish and brine in a cocktail shaker and shake vigorously.

Split between two glasses, using a fine mesh strainer to remove any pulp. Garnish with a cherry tomato and olive each.

# CHILLI

***Capsicum* species**

**Where the wild chilli came from is much debated; Bolivia, Mexico and Peru are all considered possibilities. What is undoubtedly true is that the chilli is now cultivated and eaten in many countries. It has been adopted with enthusiasm in those, and is regarded as an essential spice in a number of cuisines.**

Both colonialism and trade played a decisive part in advancing the spread of the plant. The Genoese explorer Christopher Columbus encountered chillies in Hispaniola in 1492 and introduced them to the Spanish royal court on his return from the New World. The Portuguese are credited with taking the chilli to West Africa, Southeast Asia and Goa, in India.

The chilli is the fruit of the *Capsicum* plant, with most of the chillies we grow and eat belonging to three species: *C. annuum*, *C. frutescens* and *C. chinense*. There is a huge number of cultivars that range in colour, size, shape and heat levels. The “heat” – a burning sensation felt upon contact with the mouth – is the best-known characteristic of chillies. It is created by capsaicinoids, phytochemicals designed to deter animals from eating the plant’s fruit. However – somewhat perversely – rather than being put off by the pain caused by these capsaicinoids, humans enjoy the burning sensation. Indeed, much praise is given to people who can tolerate high levels of heat, and chilli growers compete each year for the glory of growing the world’s hottest chilli pepper. Chilli heat is measured in what are called Scoville Heat Units (SHU), named after the American chemist who devised the scale.

When it comes to cooking with chillies, they are everywhere, in both fresh and dried forms: added to curries, pasta dishes, chutneys, pickles and fermented preserves such as kimchi. Chilli sauces are popular condiments, enjoyed as a simple and effective way of adding a zing to food. The Aztecs used chillies to spice their hot chocolate, a luxurious, frothy drink enjoyed by the nobility. In alcoholic drinks, chilli is used to add a piquant kick. That classic cocktail, the Bloody Mary, gets its spicy bite from a dash of Tabasco chilli sauce.

## PICANTE

(Serves 1)

2 red chilli peppers (each about ¼ inch wide)
Small handful coriander, leaves with stem
50ml tequila
1.5 tbsp runny honey
25ml fresh lime juice
Ice

**This warming tequila-based cocktail is fresh and punchy, packed with fragrant coriander. Sweeten with a good runny honey.**

—

Finely slice one chilli and press it with a muddler in a cocktail shaker. Roughly chop the coriander and place with the chilli. Add the rest of the ingredients, then shake and fine strain into an ice-filled rocks glass. Cut off the top end of the second chilli pepper and place it – stem upwards – in the drink to garnish.

# VANILLA

***Vanilla planifolia***

**One of the world's most in-demand flavourings, vanilla adds its singular fragrance to treats such as ice cream, cakes and milkshakes. So ubiquitous has it become that the word "vanilla" is now used as an adjective for something bland. But the story of vanilla is far from dull.**

This much-loved spice comes from beans found in slender pods, the fruit of the vanilla orchid (*Vanilla planifolia*). Vanilla is indigenous to Mesoamerica, where it has a storied history of culinary use; the Aztecs flavoured drinks made from cacao with it. During the sixteenth century, the Spanish introduced vanilla to Europe, whose people acquired a taste for it. Demand soared, and during the seventeenth and eighteenth centuries, colonial powers – including the British, the French, the Dutch and the Spanish – attempted to cultivate this precious spice in their tropical colonies. While vanilla vines could grow and flower in these countries, getting them to fruit and produce pods remained an elusive goal, with Mexico retaining the lucrative monopoly on vanilla cultivation for centuries. It was in 1841, on a plantation on Réunion, that an ingenious enslaved boy, 12-year-old Edmond Albius, discovered how to manually pollinate vanilla flowers and so get them to fruit. The valuable knowledge was shared among plantation owners on the island and by 1898, when production reached 200 tonnes of dried vanilla, Réunion had overtaken Mexico as a source of vanilla. The method developed by Albius is still used today.

Vanilla is sold in various forms: dried pods, bean paste, extract (made by steeping pods in alcohol) and syrup. True vanilla is expensive due to the labour involved in its production, so vanillin, a synthetic vanilla, is common in the food industry. Both vanilla and vanillin are used to infuse spirits such as vodka and rum. Its mellow, sweet notes work well with everything from chocolate and coffee to hazelnut and strawberry, making it a versatile ingredient for drink makers.

## VANILLA BEAN WHITE RUSSIAN

(Serves 1)

½ vanilla pod
50ml vodka
25ml coffee liqueur
50ml whole milk
Ice
Small grating of nutmeg, to serve (optional)

This classic, creamy cocktail bursts with fresh vanilla bean for a delicate, indulgent taste.

—

Split the vanilla pod and scrape the seeds into a cocktail shaker. Add the vodka and coffee liqueur and shake vigorously until combined. Add the milk to your glass and fill with ice. Pour over the coffee liqueur-vodka mix and stir. Finish with a fine dusting of nutmeg.

# YUZU

***Citrus × junos***

**A distinctive member of the large citrus family, the yuzu tree grew as a wild plant in Tibet and China, from where it was introduced to Japan in the Nara period (710–794 BCE).**

Unlike other citrus plants, it is resistant to cold and frost and so can be cultivated in colder climates. The tree is grown for its fruit, also called yuzu, which resembles a clementine with slightly bumpy skin that changes from green to yellow as it ripens. Japan is both the largest producer and consumer of yuzu. Seasonality is important in Japanese culture and yuzu is regarded as a winter citrus fruit. One of the customs associated with it is bathing in fresh yuzu on the eve of the winter solstice, the scent of cheesecloth-wrapped citrus perfuming the hot water.

Yuzu has a particular flavour and fragrance, described as an intriguing mixture between mandarin, lemon and grapefruit. In Japanese cuisine, where the fruit is an important ingredient, its zest, peel and juice are used in a number of ways. The grated zest is pounded with fresh green chilli and salt and fermented to make a spicy condiment called *yuzu-kosho*. Both the grated zest and the acidic juice are added to soups to enhance them, and the latter is added to salad dressings and to *ponzu*, a tart, citrus-based sauce made from yuzu and other citrus fruits. *Ponzu shoyu* (ponzu with soy sauce) is a dipping sauce accompanying dishes like sashimi or *shabu-shabu*.

As interest in the fruit builds and it enjoys a fashionable reputation outside of Japan, yuzu is being grown in countries including Australia, New Zealand, Spain and Italy. However, outside Japan, fresh yuzu fruits are rarely found, though its bottled juice, dried peel and related condiments are exported. The juice is ideal for imparting its delicate citrus notes to drink creations such as the Yuzu Sour, which is made with Japanese whisky – another export that sees high demand worldwide.

## YUZU FRENCH 75

(Serves 1)

25ml gin
10ml yuzu juice
10ml lemon juice
10ml sugar syrup
Ice
Chilled champagne, to serve
Lemon twist, to serve

**The flavour of yuzu is a hybrid between lemon and grapefruit. It is complex and moreish and works fabulously in this classic French 75, replacing some of the usual lemon juice.**

—

Pour the gin, yuzu and lemon juices and sugar syrup into a cocktail shaker with ice. Shake and pour into a chilled coupe or flute. Top with chilled fizz and garnish with a lemon twist.

# INDEX

## M



## N



## O



## P



## Q



## R

# BIBLIOGRAPHY


Grieve, M. (ed. Leyel, C.F.) (1994) *A Modern Herbal.* Tiger Books International.

Mabey, R. (1996) *Flora Britannica*. Sinclair Stevenson.

Norman, J. (2002) *Herbs & Spices*. Dorling Kindersley.

Phillips, R. & Foy, N. (1990) *Herbs*. Pan Books.

Reshi, M.H. (2017) *The Flavour of Spice*. Hachette India.

Richardson, R. (1980) *Hedgerow Cookery*. Penguin.

van Wyk, B.E. (2013) *Culinary Herbs & Spices of the World.* Kew Publishing.


# CREDITS


Photography: Laura Edwards
Food styling: Esther Clark assisted by El Kemp
Styling and art direction: Tabitha Hawkins
Design: Russell Knowles, Louise Leffler
Editorial: Isabel Wilkinson,
Caroline Curtis, Meredith Olson